Uncle Boris

Boris

in the

Yukon

and Other

Shaggy Dog Stories

Daniel Pinkwater
Illustrated by Jill Pinkwater

Simon & Schuster
New York London Toronto Sydney Singapore

🧘

SIMON & SCHUSTER
Rockefeller Center
1230 Avenue of the Americas
New York, NY 10020

SIMON & SCHUSTER and colophon are registered trademarks
of Simon & Schuster Inc.

For information about special discounts for bulk purchases,
please contact Simon & Schuster Special Sales:
1-800-456-6798 or business@simonandschuster.com

Designed by Karolina Harris

Manufactured in the United States of America

10   9   8   7   6   5   4   3   2   1

Library of Congress Cataloging-in-Publication Data is available.

ISBN 0-684-85632-8

To Jill

Uncle Boris
in the
Yukon
and Other
Shaggy Dog Stories

Chapter *1*

My father appeared to be pretty near illiterate—anyway in English. It took him a couple of hours every night to struggle his way through the newspaper, and he spoke his adopted language atrociously.

Sometimes, in order to give my father a taste of higher culture, I'd fill him in on what I was reading. Once, on a long car ride, I told him the story of Macbeth. It turned out he knew it as well as I did—better, in fact, since he appeared to remember scenes left out of my edition of the collected plays—like the one in which Macbeth's father gives his son advice, and the one in which he gives Lady Macbeth (still alive at the end of the play, as he is) a good talking-to, and she agrees to mend her ways. I tried *Hamlet, Julius Caesar,* and *King Lear,* and he knew them too, in recognizable form, but with variations that would have amazed the man from Stratford-upon-Avon. Hamlet gets married, settles down, and forgets all the nonsense; Julius Caesar retires to a resort on the Mediterranean; and Lear's children are surprised by the king's lively dance number at the end of the play.

"Dose are Jewish shows. I saw dem in Varsaw."

"You saw them in translation," I told him.

"Naw, dey vas in Yiddish. Dey vas by a Jewish writer, name of Shakespeare. I tink I knew him. I used to go to deh café vhere all deh writers vas."

"Dad, Shakespeare was English, and he lived around the end of the sixteenth century."

"I don't tink he vas det old—and English—maybe he vas, maybe he vasn't. Even your uncle used to pretend he vas an Englishman."

The uncle he referred to was Boris, the most colorful and cultured of my father's five gangster brothers from the old days in Warsaw. Boris, when he wasn't participating in holdups, dealt in objets d'art of dubious provenance. He was also the man to see if one needed documents, passports, bills of sale.

And, as I said, Boris had culture. Boris had many wealthy and prominent acquaintances, owned paintings of zaftig women with extra-bright pink nipples and fanciful ceramic sculptures in vivid polychrome, played the cello, and, from time to time, might be seen walking a borzoi, poodle, dalmatian, or some other fashionable dog in the Ogrod Saski, or Saxon Gardens, then the favorite resort of the aristocrats. He acquired, trained, and sold these dogs to the quality, and, like his other offerings, their authenticity was questionable.

Even more than my father, Boris liked to hang out with writers, and he knew a lot of them. For a long time, I assumed it was merely another manifestation of my father's craziness that he imagined he had known Shakespeare personally, but it's possible that some translators of world literature then residing in Warsaw's Yiddish district might have put it about that they were in person those authors whose works they rendered.

I could be wrong about this, but I am pretty sure that Jack London never lived upstairs over his father's tailor shop in the Stare Miasto with an angry wife and three children; nor did he pal around with my uncle Boris. But my father was convinced he had done just that.

"Sure! Who else but det Jack London talked your uncle into going to Alyeska?"

These were the serene days of a Warsaw now barely remembered, of lime trees and cafés on Ujazdowska Alesa Avenue, vendors, musicians, and street characters in Sigismund Square. I imagine my father, a healthy young hoodlum, promenading in the Krasinski Gardens.

He and his brothers were Jewish thugs, and it was a point of pride that they were more cultivated and showed more style than the Poles who followed the same profession.

I have a photograph of my father and his brothers in those days. They are manicured and pomaded, holding whangee canes and kidskin gloves, wearing flash neckties, and staring into the camera with the expression of cape buffalo contemplating a tourist.

The enterprise of my father and my five uncles was that of hijacking goods from express wagons, then ransoming them back to their consignors according to a strict schedule of fees. Anyone declining to redeem his merchandise would begin a run of bad luck requiring doctors, the fire brigade, or even the rabbinate—but since everybody was familiar with the system, serious mishaps were generally avoided.

The brothers did well. They were treated with respect, and their earnings were above average; they wore snappy clothes, acquired such art objects as they were able to appreciate, attended the finest brothels, and knew everybody.

Including Jack London (aka Ossip Weintraub, the tailor's son), author of *The Call of the Wild*, known locally as *A Ruf Fun der Vildernish*. The adventure writer and political radical fascinated Boris, and they frequently spent long nights drinking wine and yearning for the life of the trail and the land of the midnight sun.

Before long, Boris was suffering from Klondike fever, gold madness, wanderlust, and itchy feet. Encouraged by London, who would have gone with him, were he not facing a deadline for *White Fang*, or *Der Vyser Tzon*, Boris set out for the Yukon.

The story of Boris's journey from Warsaw to Moscow, from Gorky to Sverdlovsk, from Omsk to Novosibirsk, from Krasnoyarsk to Irkutsk, then to Ulaan-baatar, Tientsin, Mukden, Harbin, and finally to Vladi-vostok, has been told and retold in my family ever since he made it. Each teller has emphasized those aspects important to him or her. It was my mother who told me the story—apparently my ordinarily taciturn father had let loose at some point and related it—so what I know about Boris's crossing of the Russo-Siberian landmass, plus chunks of Mongolia and China, is that he consumed nothing but tea and dry toast the whole way, and never once used a public toilet.

It was Boris himself who told me what happened after he took ship to Juneau. When I knew him, Boris was an old man. He spent most of his time in an over-heated room full of garish ceramics. I remember him, resembling Erich von Stroheim, wearing a silk dressing gown, smoking yellow Sobranie "Chaliapin" cigarettes, and drinking cup after cup of tea from an ormolu samovar. It was hard to imagine him as a sourdough and dog-musher, but this is the story he told me.

"On deh ship ve vas playing cards a lot. Mostly I remember euchre and klaviash ve played. I vas a good player, and I made it a lot of money. So vhen I'm landing in Juneau, I got vhat ve calling a 'grubstake.' By dis I'm going to a nice hotel, vit a hot bath is extra a dollar, and I'm having a bath, and by a barber a haircut and a shave, and in deh hotel I'm eating corned beef vit potatoes, and I'm tinking vhat I'm going to do next.

"So vhile I'm sitting, comes in deh only Jewish gold

miner in deh whole Alyeska, by deh name Jacob Grossberg, but dey calling him 'deh Kootenai Yid.' So deh
Yid sees me, I'm putting a potato in mine mouth, and he
says, 'Hey, boychik! Dis a long vay frum deh shtetl.'

"So I answer him, 'I ain't no farm boy, mister.' At dis
time, I don't know he's deh Kootenai Yid, but anyways
I'm polite, because it always pays you show respect,
never knowing maybe dis individual is in a bad mood
and he pulls out a pistol and shoots a couple holes in
you, just he should feel better. So I'm calling deh Yid
mister, and he throws a leg over a chair and puts me deh
qvestion, 'So, Yankel, you came by vay frum Noo
Yawk?'

" 'No sir,' I tell deh Yid. 'I'm here frum Poland, deh
hard vay. My name ain't Yankel, and please do me deh
honor I should buy you a slug vhiskey.'

"So I can see right avay, Jacob Grossberg, deh Kootenai Yid, is sizing me up, and vhat he sees, he likes. 'So
vhat could you did so bad in Poland det you hev to
come all deh vay to Alyeska?'

" 'I'll tell you, mister,' I say. 'I didn't do nawting so
bad. I vas in business vit mine brothers back in Varsaw,
and I came to Alyeska to see vhat's vhat.'

" 'So vhat business?' deh Yid asks.

" 'Removals,' I answer him right back.

" 'Is det like, I hev something waluable, you remove
it?'

" 'Exact,' I tell him.

" 'And vhat if I don't vant you should remove?'

" 'Den I'm persuading.'

" 'And vhat argument you gonna persuade vit?'

" 'Deh best.'

"So vitout no more ado, I go to work for deh Kootenai Yid. I'm protecting his gold, and he is loining me deh vays of deh Northland."

Apparently, Boris did a number of distinctly odd jobs for Jacob Grossberg and earned the approval—or at least the respect—of the hard-bitten and frostbitten community, and the soubriquet "Warsaw Willy."

"Never give your right name on deh road," Boris told me.

After about a year, Boris said good-bye to the Kootenai Yid, bought a team of Malamutes and the rest of a prospector's outfit, and set out to strike it rich on his own.

Paydirt eluded Boris. In a number of forays up the Chilkoot, he prospected extensively in the Yukon Territory and found no gold. After each unsuccessful attempt, he'd amass another grubstake, reprovision, and try again.

Needless to say, Boris had become expert at living rough and, like many of the sourdoughs, was more at ease on the trail than in town. As Boris told the story, at a certain point he had more or less given up the idea of striking gold, but continued to prospect simply because it was the most agreeable thing to do.

Boris had learned to anticipate changes in weather by a thousand signs. A sudden squall could be fatal. He had learned to judge the condition of snow on the trail by sight, touch, smell, and taste. If he fell into freezing water, he could strip and dress himself in dry gear, thus saving his life, while keeping his team in harness and moving. And he was able to make first-class pastrami from caribou meat.

So it was that Boris found himself, many days from any sign of human life, enjoying a campfire and the company of his dogs, when Jake spoke to him.

Jake, a large brown Malamute, had been Boris's lead dog from the beginning. Jake had selected himself for this position of honor and responsibility in the usual way—by intimidating the other dogs. Some dogs are cut out to be leaders, and some are not; and if a dog is anything else, as the saying goes, the view never changes. Where Jake differed from the standard "alpha," or executive-type dog, was in his affability and abundant charm. Even when chewing to rags another dog who had given in to the inborn prompting to test Jake's authority, Jake appeared bemused, even kindly. And he never held a grudge—Jake would often show solicitude or affection to the dog he had just fanged, shredded, and de-eared.

A dog like this becomes a real colleague and helper to the musher, and can enjoy a status midway between dog and human. Jake was not tethered at night, as the rest of the team was. He would have his evening meal out of a tin pan with Boris, beside the campfire, after the other dogs had been tossed their hunks of frozen

fish. The last sight Boris would see from within his sleeping robe at night, and the first sight he would see in the morning, would be Jake lying nearby, gazing out into the dark or the distance, alert to possible danger.

It is certain that the instant Jake knew Boris was unconscious, he himself would drop off and sleep like a stone, waking up ten seconds before his master—he also stole food, feigned affection, and did all the things dogs have done over the millennia to get in tight with the boss. Notwithstanding, Jake was as good as dogs get, and Boris, in the habit of carrying on one-sided conversations with him, became only incrementally aware that the dog was answering.

On this particular occasion, Boris tossed Jake the heel of a hunk of moose salami on which he'd been gnawing. "Dos iz far eich,"[1] Boris said. "A klainer ondenk."[2]

"Ir zeit zaier gut-hartsik,"[3] Jake responded.

"Es iz be'emes gornisht,"[4] Boris said.

A silence followed. Both chewed their salami. Boris finally muttered, "Der hund ret. Ver volt dos geglaibt?"[5]

"Ruft mich ziben a zaiger in der fri,"[6] Jake said, and closed his eyes.

---

1. This is for you.
2. A little souvenir.
3. You are very kind.
4. It's nothing, really.
5. The dog spoke. Who would have believed it?
6. Call me at seven A.M.

In the days that followed, Jake's command of Yiddish changed his relationship with Boris, expectably. The dog could not only speak; he could sing "Rumania, Rumania," and he could tell a joke. Some dogs can tell a joke—some dogs can't.

It wasn't long before Boris concluded that he'd discovered something more valuable than gold. He and the dog decided that they would head for civilization and capitalize on Jake's talent.

Months later, they hit New York and found their way to a tiny shared office in a shabby Midtown building where a booking agent named D. Isayevitch secured them a spot on the Hebrew Orpheum circuit, following a harlequinade entitled "Shapiro and Shapirette."

Their own act, Isayevitch had named "Boris and Maurice, the Golden Fools." This was a set piece with a Klondike motif. Jake, as Maurice, was dressed in a little suit of clothes and sat at a table, playing cards and wisecracking with Boris. The act failed to click. The suit of clothes detracted from the novelty of Jake as a talking dog, and audiences assumed he was either a man disguised as a dog or simply a very ugly man.

Boris was undistinguished as a straight man, and Jake's talent alone was insufficient to put the act over. His voice was raspy and did not carry well, and his material, developed with Boris's help and the advice of Isayevitch the booking agent, was second-rate.

But it was technology that hastened the demise of Boris and Maurice. Advances in the phonograph industry dealt a staggering blow to Yiddish vaudeville. People stayed away in droves, listening to "Cohen on the Telephone" in the privacy of their own homes.

Canceled in Harrisburg, Pennsylvania, Boris had to wire Isayevitch for the fare back to New York, and pawn Jake's suit for the price of a hot meal and a couple of nights in a Bowery flophouse.

"Der glaykhster veg iz ful mit shteyner,"[7] Jake said, and therewith abandoned speaking in the tongue of humans.

Eventually, Boris resumed his old trade of faking antiques, and lived modestly with Jake in the Flatbush section of Brooklyn. They were a regular sight on fine Sunday afternoons in Prospect Park, the old sled dog and the middle-aged forger, making their weekly promenade with solemn dignity.

Jake, having chosen the life of a normal canine, steadfastly refused to utter a word. He padded along at Boris's side, permitted the children of Brooklyn to pet him and pull his ears, and even exchanged correct sniffs with ordinary dogs of the borough, none of whom were capable of appreciating what he was and what he had been.

At the last, Jake spoke—remarkably, in English. Just before taking his final leave, Jake raised his head and said to his old companion of the trail, "If Isayevitch, that putz, hadn't dressed me up in the damned suit, we would have had a shot at the big time."

---

7. The smoothest way is full of stones.

Chapter 2

All his life my father was in love with Warsaw, where he was born, survived childhood, and became a gangster. While talking on the telephone, he would endlessly doodle on his scratch pad, "Warszawa, Warszawa, Warszawa," embellishing and overscoring the letters until they shone out darkly on the white paper. He'd also mutter about Warsaw in his sleep.

He never described it, but the way he'd inscribe the name of his lost city caused me, as a child, to picture it as a place of sunshine, flowers, music, public parks, and good things to eat. Which apparently it was before, and for a time after, the lamps went out all over Europe.

I've seen Warsaw only once, during a dark and snowy, bitter-cold February in 1960. Those buildings that had survived the war were pocked with patched bullet holes, and the ones built since then all resembled federal post offices. Here and there I was able to find a portion of a street or an intersection where, by masking the adjacent horrible blocks of flats with my hands, I could make a picture that evoked the former capital, said to be the Paris of Eastern Europe.

I was with my father on that trip—his last trip anywhere. He was not seeing the gray earthbound monstrosities, or the vacancy that replaced the ghetto. He stood on empty ground and counted houses that were not there, pointing out to me where he had been born, a certain restaurant, his school, and all those places where he and his brothers had lived and fought and stolen and celebrated. And in part through his vision, I saw it too, superimposed on the wintry postwar dreariness.

It's hard to say whether old Warsaw was really that lovable a place, or just a warm memory in contrast with the unimagined harshness of the immigrant experience. It's a fact that the bulk of popular entertainment enjoyed by newly arrived residents of the Lower East Side of New York was heavy with nostalgia for the old home. There was no end to the songs about villages and towns where the Jews had starved, and from which they had departed just in front of the hooves of Cossack horses.

When asked about this, my father responded that feeling homesick for nine tenths of the shtetls of Eastern Europe was similar to yearning for a double dose of cholera, but that Warsaw was something else again. Other towns were puddles, Budapest was a sham, Paris a mockery. Warsaw was the goods, a paradise on earth.

And yet he left it. As to why, I got the occasional hint from the rare enigmatic and fragmentary remark uttered by my father, such as "Vhen I vas in Poland, I vas deh only vun of mine brudders det didn't carry a pistol."

"And why was that?" I might have asked. "Why didn't you carry a pistol?"

"Because I vas so tough I didn't need it, a pistol," my father might have answered.

"And why did your brothers carry pistols?"

"Did you did your homework? Go! Study alraddy!"

Another clue comes from an old photo: my grandparents and their children. He is a small man with wide-set eyes—a shoo-in for the part of Papa, had he ever tried out for the Yiddish stage adaptation of *The Brothers Karamazov*. Impressive as he is, Grandpa is completely eclipsed by Grandma, a woman displaying a strong right arm, and frightening, even in a photograph. In the picture, my grandmother sits a little apart, with a glint in her eye the likes of which I hope never to see in real life. My guess is that members of the community were able to imagine that the consequences dealt out by the brothers should they, the regular citizens, fail to stand and deliver, would be nothing compared to what the holdupniks were used to getting at home.

One version of the story of my father's decision to emigrate goes that his fare to America was raised by subscription, and that a number of decent citizens armed themselves and escorted him to the train early one morning. They bought him candy and magazines and reminded him never to return.

So it came to pass that my father, a vigorous young brute bearing a beautiful handmade passport (a present from his brother Boris), arrived in vigorous and brutal New York City in the early 1920s.

Nobody hits New York and immediately takes it by storm, no matter how tough a tough guy or how smart an operator one was in one's hometown. The competition has always been fierce—new talent is always arriving in the ultimate border town, and everybody is part of the food chain.

Thus my father strolled down the gangplank, serene that his various talents would see him through, and was reduced to a bum in a matter of days.

On board ship, individuals could be found from whom the immigrant might, for a modest sum, borrow a roll of bills sufficient to satisfy the inspectors at Ellis Island that said immigrant would not starve in the streets. Once my father had survived the terrifying examination process and passed through the turnstile, he handed back his rented bankroll and boarded the launch for New York City with two dollars and forty-five cents in his pocket.

My father once told me that the feature that most impressed him in the first minutes in his new country was the size of the average New York City policeman. He was discarding options for his immediate survival.

By the time I got to know my father, he was a paradigm of honesty and rectitude. I never knew the professional holdupnik. Something had happened to change him. It may have been the occasion when two earlier arrivals, guys in the same line of work who knew him from the other side, held a pistol to each of his temples and spoke discouraging words.

My father entered into the bedrock, bare-knuckles immigrant experience. His early efforts at survival in America consisted of schnorring the price of a sandwich from people who had arrived a few weeks earlier, picking up odd day jobs, and sleeping in parked cars at night. He ascended from sleeping in parked cars to dreadful rented rooms, from sweeping out butcher shops on a per diem basis to making regular deliveries for a bootlegger, and on up the ladder.

But not very far up the ladder did my father go, and not very fast. Years passed, and he was still living out of a cardboard suitcase and sleeping in cheap rooms.

"I vas lying on mine back, vatching deh bugs march across deh ceiling, and I took stock frum mine life. By dis time dere vasn't nawting I didn't do it . . . tvice. And at eferyting I failed. Vhy vas det? I decided it vas because all deh time tings vould get lousy, I vould make a change. Dis time, I vas gonna pick someting and just do it—vedder a success or a failure, I vas just gonna keep on vit it. And I picked . . . regs. I was gonna buy regs, and sall regs, and tink regs, and talk regs, and eat regs, and sleep regs until I made it of mineself someting."

Rags. Old clothes. Remnants, oddments, bits, and scraps. Fibers to be recycled in the manufacture of fine paper, new cloth, industrial wipers. And rags as clothing.

Ever wonder where the natives in the pathetic and impoverished countries get their rags? In the prosperous industrial West, the pauperage could get its rags in the form of cast-offs from the well-to-do, but what of those places too poor to support an overclass large enough to discard sufficient quantities for the general population? Those rags were imported in great bales. At the quayside or railhead in Oran, Marangu, or Tonganoxie, the bales would be cut open on the spot, and the locals would bid for wearables and then troop off proudly to have their picture taken by *National Geographic.*

Of course, my father did not go overnight from watching the wallpaper-bug parade to scrap-fiber magnate and rag merchant to the elite—but he did make some progress. Modest progress. He came to possess a used Dodge, a permanent business establishment in a bad part of Memphis, Tennessee, and an American wife—a widow of reasonable quality, down on her luck.

* * *

Expecting the arrival of what turned out to be me, my parents fixed up an apartment in a building with not too many rats, and worked hard to make such a home as they were able to imagine for the fledgling family. The little rag shop prospered, or at least did not fail. They owned a radio. Survival seemed probable.

Whereupon Uncle Boris arrived in Memphis with a present: a Pekingese dog. Boris was a great one for imaginative gifts. Throughout his life, he would surprise relatives, distant relatives, and those who had not known they were relatives with exotic pieces of ceramic art sent by post. When they responded with a note of thanks, he would surprise them again with a bill.

The Pekingese was not made of ceramic. It was a real dog. Uncle Boris, a lifelong dog fancier, had made a profitable sideline of faking and selling purebreds. He had once traveled all the way from Poland to Austria to deliver, it is believed, a black chow chow, or something resembling a chow chow, to no less a person than Sigmund Freud. It isn't certain that it was Freud, but a photograph taken on the occasion shows someone who might be Freud, Boris, and the dog, all three arranged on a settee, looking happily into the camera. Uncle Boris's recollection was only of "a big Jewish doctor in Vienna." He remembered the dog very well.

If the man in the photo is Freud, I can hardly imagine that, having met Boris, he did not at least make some notes on him. They would have conversed in Yiddish, and as voluble as Boris was, Freud would have had to notice that he had come across a treasure-house of abnormality. However, my letters to the Freud Archives have gone unanswered, so there is no telling whether the historic meeting actually took place. Perhaps the

Master was distracted by the puppy and thus missed a chance to advance the new science and make money by analyzing Boris.

Boris's gift to my mother and father was Bobby, a frisky little fellow who won everyone's heart and made puddles on the floor. Old snapshots suggest that the dog really was a Pekingese, or mostly so—a little on the ugly side—but that would have served only to endear Bobby to my father and uncle. They shared a love of the grotesque in decor and pets. Monkeys, colorful parrots, miniature horses, teacup poodles, and anything bow-legged, bug-eyed, dwarfed, or unnatural excited them and conformed to their ideas of high style and gracious living.

"A dog like dis is all deh rage in deh best parts of Brooklyn," Boris told his brother.

To an extent, Bobby eclipsed the next big moment in the life of the family, which was my arrival. Dogs are more fun than newborns, and the stories I was told later in childhood about my first days on earth did not have me as the subject. However, I felt no resentment toward Bobby—and, as will become clear, he was anything but jealous of me.

I think it is relatively unlikely that my parents might have eaten me. Had they done so, it would have to have been by mistake. This having been said, it needs to be noted that something of the kind was not absolutely out of the question given the sort of parents my parents were.

From the day I was brought home, Bobby appointed himself my protector. During that vulnerable period in which I was not dissimilar to a meat loaf, he lurked under my crib, growled, and challenged anyone who came near me; on those occasions when adults handled me, he kept a watchful and unmistakably threatening eye on them. Bobby was ultimately judged incorrigible and given away, but not before seeing me through the edible stage.

If one is going to grow up in a certain kind of family—I like to think of it as precivilized—it's a good thing to have some basis for understanding it early. The story of Bobby provided me with a tiny foothold. In contemplating why he may have thought I needed protection in the first place, I took my first childlike steps toward useful insights.

All my life, I have wondered what became of Bobby. In retrospect, I developed a feeling for him like that which one might have for a lost twin. He had seen me through the first dangerous months of life—and would have stuck with me longer if he had been able.

I salute you, Bobby, my brother, long ago subsumed into the cosmic pool of dog soul. I've done my best to keep faith with you through subsequent avatars of that spirit. You, and the other dogs, taught me what I needed to know about becoming a human being.

Chapter **3**

The wartime boom catapulted my father to the top of his profession. Heavy with rag wealth, we emigrated to Chicago and a vast ten-room apartment on the North Side. Built after the great fire but before the end of the gaslight era, such dwellings are common in Chicago.

Our apartment was on the top floor of a three-story brick building and had an open porch, plus a glassed-in solarium at each end. Big as it was, it seemed even bigger to a little kid, and together with the dirt and concrete backyard, and the park just down the block, it constituted my whole world for a number of years.

Each of my parents had a son and a daughter from a previous marriage, and both had solved the problems of single parenthood by tossing their kids into orphanages: another example of the like-mindedness that made their marriage such a success. My father's children, Jack and Elaine, had graduated from their respective asylums by the time we hit Chicago, and were both married and launching dysfunctional families of their own. My mother's kids, Milo and Inga, were high-schoolers and lived with us in the big apartment.

My father had quaint and antique European notions about the status of stepchildren, which might have caused friction had my mother not agreed with them. Thus, Milo slept in the tiny room intended for the maid, and made himself useful with floor scrubbing, ceiling washing, and similar domestic tasks, while Inga, full-time unpaid baby-sitter, shared a room with dear little me.

It would have been understandable if Milo and Inga had resented me. I rated, after all, as a person—and they were only step-persons. But they had been taught humane values in the orphanage and were happy to look after their baby half brother. My mother and father were busy getting and spending, enjoying the exhilarating social scene in wartime Chicago. My father would leave for work early—I never saw him mornings. After breakfast, my mother would leave me under the supervision of the hired girl and head for the department stores in the Loop. In the afternoon, Milo and Inga would return from high school and take me out for an airing, do their homework, and prepare the evening meal, which we would eat together. My parents would return to the apartment in time to change into glad rags, then depart for socializing and night-clubbing. I would be half awakened at one in the morning by my parents visiting my room. I remember my mother's hugs, her fur coat frigid and bristling with the Chicago night air, and her cheek cold against mine. My father was perceived as a glowing cigarette end in the darkness.

In the morning, I would be presented with eight-by-ten glossy photographs of my father and mother, seated at tables with other identical couples: blue-jawed, gold-toothed, broken-nosed men in splendid suits, and pneumatic women in furs. These were souvenirs taken by the camera girls at various nightclubs—and I had an extensive collection, along with decorative swizzle sticks with the names of the clubs printed on them.

Most of my time was spent with Milo and Inga. They did a decent job of seeing me through my early childhood. Inga read to me a lot. She didn't have much patience with kiddie books and selected stuff that would interest us both. She tended toward literature and art history, and I clearly remember poring over color plates of the work of Velázquez with Inga at a time before I was proficient at buttoning my own clothes. Van Loon's history of art kept us both busy for a long time, and I knew *Tom Sawyer* and *Huckleberry Finn* before I could read them—and later, when I could read, I read them. I have never felt disadvantaged by missing *Winnie-the-Pooh* and *Uncle Wiggly* at an age when they might have made God knows what impression on me.

Milo was concentrated on being an outdoorsman, man's man, and adventurer. He told me many stories about hunting and fishing, neither of which he had done yet, but I was convinced he had bagged many a grizzly and mountain sheep. He also related the plots of movies he'd seen, most of which had to do with spies, private detectives, and acts of personal heroism.

Milo was also interested in science and technology, and built a superheterodyne radio set and many model airplanes with me hovering at his elbow.

From time to time, Uncle Boris occupied the other back bedroom. He didn't go to work and spent his days around the apartment, tinkering with cinema equipment.

Uncle Boris claimed to have been the first private person in Poland to own a movie camera—or he might have meant that he was the first Jew to do so. Whoever had sold him the camera had apparently instructed him to always include the feet of his subject, doubtless meaning that Boris should photograph from sufficient distance to show the whole figure, head to toe.

Boris interpreted this differently and thus came upon what was to be his cinematic signature, the long pan, down the body to the shoes, where the shot lingered.

As Boris's technique expanded, he devised lateral pans of the feet of a number of people sitting on a sofa, tracking shots of the feet of three or four people abreast, walking toward the camera along the sidewalk, and low-angle shots of dancing feet.

My favorites of Uncle Boris's films were those in which I appeared. There were many reels of me as a cute little kid being swung through the air by tough-

looking men in tight-fitting overcoats with wide shoulder pads and snap-brim hats. These were my father, uncle, and eldest brother, Jack—looking like gangsters, although they were now all more or less honest ragmen and dealers in various kinds of scrap material.

Boris's great work was a collaboration with my father, who was Boris's disciple in the art of cinema and was himself a proponent of the foot shot. The two of them converted our dining room into an editing room and spent a number of weeks cutting all the foot footage out of the family films and splicing them into a two-hour epic entitled "Feet."

They would show the film every time they got a chance, excitedly encouraging the viewers to guess whose feet they were looking at. "Look! Whose feets is that? Nah! Wrong! It's Aunt Sadie's feets!" They loved that film. It was an interactive art experience.

* * *

Milo yearned for a dog. He saw himself making his way through fields of frosty stubble, his shotgun broken over his arm, with a noble bird dog by his side. The fact that he'd probably never seen a field of frosty stubble, and that his shotgun was a relic of the previous century and missing some of its working parts, did not deter him in the least. One day when I knocked at the door of his room, an arm shot out of the adjacent tiny second bathroom, and I was yanked within and simultaneously hushed.

"See what I've got!" Milo whispered.

The bathroom was steamy and smelled of something wonderful, which turned out to be flea soap. Looming in the bathtub was a solemn Irish setter, patiently holding still while Milo scrubbed him.

"His name is Stan," Milo said. "You can touch him. See how gentle he is?"

I reached out a hand and felt the soaking fur of Stan's throat. He gave my arm a deferential dab with his tongue. I looked into his eyes. They were brimming with pure love.

"Where did he come from?" I asked Milo. We were still whispering.

"I bought him," Milo said. "He's a real hunting dog. Stan and I are going to get some ducks this year, aren't we, Stan?"

Stan stoically continued to endure his bath.

"Do they know you have him?" I asked.

"When they see what a good dog he is, it'll be all right," Milo said. "I'll take good care of him."

Milo allowed me to help towel-dry Stan, and we all crowded into Milo's room. Stan stretched out on the braided rag rug and permitted us to admire him.

Stan was not a young dog. His muzzle was grizzled with white. He was content to snooze in Milo's room, calmly ate a can of Strongheart dog food, and dutifully relieved himself when taken to the backyard. All of which Milo and I thought was wonderful.

Inga was not impressed by Stan's presence and retired to her closet to do her homework. This was the closet of the bedroom I shared with her, and it had an electric light. She spent the bulk of her evenings there, sitting on an old trunk, reading, and writing with her Parker fountain pen, a gift from the staff at the orphanage. Even at hours when I had not yet gone to bed and there was no need to keep the room dark, and even when the apartment was mostly empty and she might have used any of the rooms to study, she gravitated to her closet.

On the evening of Stan's arrival, I remained in Milo's room until late. We listened to *The Shadow* on the superheterodyne and talked quietly across the sleeping dog. His fur had dried to a deep russet, and he smelled of the marvelous flea soap.

Stan allowed me to curl up on the rug beside him, and there I fell asleep. Milo must have carried me to my room.

In the middle of the night, my parents came in. My mother's mink cape, smelling of perfume and cigarette smoke, was nothing like the setter's warm coat.

"You'll let Milo keep Stan, won't you?" I muttered sleepily, my arms around my mother's neck.

In the morning, I awoke in a state of joy and high excitement. I dashed to Milo's room. Neither Milo nor Stan was there. Milo had gone out and taken Stan with him.

I thought of nothing but Stan all day. I told myself a hundred stories about Stan, and all the things we would do together, until I believed we had done them. I made up games that Stan would like, set aside toys for him to play with, and conceived arguments that would persuade Milo to allow Stan to sleep in my room sometimes.

When Milo returned late in the afternoon, he was alone. He went directly to his room and locked the door. I knocked on the door, but he did not answer. It would be days before he spoke to anyone in the apartment. He would never say another word about Stan, and no one would ever tell me what had happened to him.

Inga found me, I don't know how much later, sitting on the floor outside Milo's locked door, drenched with tears.

Chapter 4

Milo had failed to work Stan into the family, but he had had an unexpected effect. Now my father was thinking about getting a family pet.

My father's idea of modernity consisted of decorating in pale colors, lots of free-form lamps made of driftwood, and exotic animals. Chihuahuas, iguanas, parrots, and especially monkeys intrigued him. For a long time, he would keep me abreast of his progress in securing a monkey.

"Ven I vas in New York lest veek, I saw a monkey no bigger dan dis finger," he would tell me. "Just before deh train vas leaving, I vent to deh pet shop, but alraddy he vas gone. Next time, I promise."

I was never sure how to respond to these reports. First there was his joyous enthusiasm at the idea of bringing home a monkey. And as a kid, I had a natural curiosity about, and automatic liking for, all animals. But somehow I sensed that, as a pet, a monkey might be a source of misery. I have since learned that this is usually the case from a hundred stories too dreadful to tell here.

Happily, none of the stories is firsthand. It was a parrot my father brought home when he finally took the plunge.

Right after World War II, very few people in Chicago had parrots, and there wasn't a whole lot known about their care—or where to get one. My father got one, a double yellow head Panama named Pedro. I was afraid of him.

Anyone acquainted with parrots will tell you they're crazy. Intelligent, yes. Affectionate. But also psychotic. Pedro was a self-contained sort of bird who would tear anyone approaching him to shreds—except my father, of course. He loved my father.

After spending a day amusing himself by vocalizing insanely and tossing sunflower-seed shells in a nine-foot radius around his perch, Pedro would sense my father's imminent arrival home from work. Pedro knew when my father was precisely thirty minutes from the front door. At this point he would begin crowing and cooing insistently. This performance would accelerate until he was shrieking and convulsing, flapping and hyperventilating. By the time my father actually came through the door, Pedro would have worked himself into a fit. His feathers awry, his pupils dilating and contracting, he'd be hanging upside down, gripping his perch with one zygodactylous claw.

My father would have to gather Pedro up and cradle him in his arms, arranging his feathers and comforting him, while Pedro made deranged croaking noises.

Weekends, my father would hang around the house in his underwear. If visitors came, he would put his pants on—if they were friends of his—if not, not. Pedro had the freedom of the house. He would come careening out of the dining room (Pedro was not a good flier) and land on my father, powerful talons wrapping around his clavicle and a trickle of blood appearing on his undershirt. My father would stroke Pedro.

"Det's a good boid," he would say, "a good boid."

Pedro fell ill. There wasn't a vet in all of Chicago who dealt with parrots. Besides, it was too cold to risk taking him outside, had there been anywhere to take him. We phoned the zoo vet, who said it sounded like pneumonia. Keep him warm and give him stimulants.

A cruel fate caused the boiler to quit during Pedro's crisis. Everybody moved into the kitchen to keep warm. My father stayed home from work to nurse him. I remember coming home from school to find this scene: Pedro was wrapped in a dish towel. To immobilize him, my father had made a sort of cradle out of one of those black enamel oval roasting pans. He had Pedro resting on the open oven door and was in the process of pouring a shot of Ballentine's Scotch down his beak. Pedro was looking around wildly. What could he have been thinking?

I figure the bird died of fear as much as anything else.

This was the first time I had encountered death. Pedro, who, when alive, had been nothing but a noisy lunatic, cackling to himself and making a tremendous mess, appeared sweet and angelic when dead. I believe I revised my whole experience of him in an instant. I took it hard that he had, so to speak, croaked, as did my father. We spent a long time sitting in the darkened living room, grieving. It was the first time I had seen my father express a human emotion, albeit not for a human. This moment of bonding had an unlooked-for result.

"Sonnyeh," my father said, sniffing, "don't you vorry, boy. We'll hev more parrots—lots of parrots."

I felt a little flutter of terror, not quite on the level of that which I'd felt when he talked about monkeys—but the monkey had never materialized—now he was talking about a whole lot of parrots, and we'd already had one.

"Or maybe we'll just get a dog?" I whimpered, snuggling up to my father.

"Naw, Sonnyeh, you don't hev to sattle for a dog. I'll get you planty parrots, vait and see."

So my father and I now had a hobby in common. This meant that I would read aloud to him from a book called *Psittacine Family Birds,* and he would acquire such birds, and we would care for them, and they would bite me.

I became fairly proficient in dealing with foot scale, bird mites, wing clipping, creating nutritious mixtures of seeds and grain, and the many psychological disorders peculiar to parrots, including the common one of neurotically plucking out their own feathers until they look like dressed chickens on the hoof.

To this day, I have a way with parrots, and sometimes I will take a friend into a pet shop where I can show off by relating to the birds, calming the frantic ones, getting others to talk and coo suggestively and offer their heads to be scratched. I have even picked up my father's trick—for which my hands were too small in the old days—of taking a punishing beak between my knuckles and engaging in a kind of tug-of-war, which they seem to appreciate.

None of this should be taken to suggest that I like parrots, macaws, cockatoos, cockatiels, parakeets, lorikeets, African lovebirds, or any of that disagreeable bunch; nor have I ever liked them. My idea of cruel and unusual punishment is to be confined with a parrot— hell would be confinement with a whole lot of them. All my life, I've pretty much avoided most southerly places, especially Australia, those being places where hook-billed seedeaters fly wild.

But as a child, I was scarcely aware that I possessed an indifference to parrots that I would later realize masked aversion. Parrot culture was an activity I shared with my father, a personage with whom I previously had nothing in common, and who had heretofore been a complete mystery to me. How many kids have ritually endured Little League baseball and bone-threatening PeeWee football for similar reasons?

At the height of the parrot craze, my parents discovered a new direction to travel for pleasure. At the onset of winter, we would entrain for California. On these trips, my sister Inga was included in the role of nanny.

The family must have made an unforgettable picture as we made ready to board the Super Chief in Chicago. A single-file procession: first my father, wearing his powder-blue suit, Stetson, and topcoat and carrying, over his shoulder, the brown leather case containing his Cine-Kodak and, in hand, a huge Zenith portable radio in the shape of a suitcase, featuring the patented Wave Magnet antenna. My mother would follow in her fur-piece, clutching a few magazines. Next in line, myself, bearing two wooden traveling cases full of parakeets, and bringing up the rear, looking as though she wanted to die, Inga, bearing another box containing a parrot or two.

My father would have booked a double drawing room, and once we were rolling, we would spread out and get comfortable. The powerful Zenith would be fired up and the Wave Magnet stuck to the window with suction cups so we could listen to H. V. Kaltenborn, *It Pays to Be Ignorant,* and other favorites. My father would relax behind a newspaper. The traveling boxes would be opened, and the birds would flutter and perch about the compartment. I would sprawl on the floor, absorbed in a comic. My mother might knit, and Inga would fixate on the pages of *Gardner's Art Through the Ages,* probably fantasizing that she was traveling in another country, and alone. Pullman porters would bring ice-cold 7UP, the family's favorite traveling beverage. And so we would rattle through the night, oblivious (except for Inga) of our oddness, heading for a winter beneath the palms.

In time, the parrot craze diminished. The parakeets and lesser Psittaciformes went, I know not where. They may have died off or been given away, I don't recall. We wound up with one parrot, Lucky—a fairly mellow Panama, by far the least obnoxious of all the birds we'd owned. My father left Lucky in the care of his daughter, Elaine, who now lived in California, when we left for Chicago at the end of one winter. Elaine hung Lucky's cage on her patio, and one day he picked the lock and headed for Mexico.

"God bless him," Inga said when we got the news. "I hope he makes it."

Chapter 5

"So dis time," my father said, "instead ve go to California for deh vinter, ve just go poimanent."

And within two weeks, my mother had canceled the lease, engaged movers, sold the furniture, including the two Baldwin uprights, and we were on our way.

The reason we had two pianos was that my father had been offered a deal too good to pass up. My mother played a little—the only member of the family to do so, but had Jascha Zayde and Leonid Hambro turned up, itching to render a double Mondschein Sonata, we could have accommodated them.

Inga was to accompany us to California and finish high school there. For Milo, my father had a more original plan. In another example of charming Europeanness and nineteenth-century-ism, my father appears to have indentured Milo to his friend Horowitz—the only man who spoke with the same nearly incomprehensible accent as my father and, needless to say, was a completely annoying person.

We arrived in California—my mother and father, Inga and I, and a few parrots. I missed Milo. I thought he had been given a raw deal. I didn't know yet that I was going to military school.

They enrolled me in an academy known as Golden Military Institute. The school slogan was "Honor, Duty, Country, Remedial Algebra."

My assumption is that my father wanted me educated with the ruling class. My mother liked the uniforms, and to be fair to Colonel Golden, at $575, it was the best-made suit of clothes I've ever owned.

My parents saved money by sending me as a day student, which meant I was spared the agony of dorm life, but also that I was not fully accepted by the other little cadets.

I noticed that the life of the civilian children in my neighborhood revolved around bicycles and dogs. Gangs of them would mount up and, with their pooches galloping alongside, take off for who knew what fun. I had neither bicycle nor dog, and the kids identified me as a private school elitist snob and militarist, so naturally they shunned me.

Every afternoon I would hop off the blue school bus and settle down for a fantasy fix. My favorite TV program then—and to this day—was the afternoon Western hosted by Colonel Tim McCoy USA, Retired. Tim McCoy was a genuine cowboy, a student of Indian sign language, and a historian of the Old West; he had seen out the last of the horse cavalry during World War I, had been a movie star, and was the handsomest man who ever lived. McCoy had personally met desperadoes, lawmen, and formerly hostile Indian chiefs, and he knew the real story about everything. During breaks in the movie, he would fill in the audience vis-à-vis reality versus Hollywood, demonstrate authentic six-gun technique (sneak up from behind), explain trick riding, and share his collection of photos of badmen of the West, usually on mortuary slabs with lots of holes in them.

While warming up for the colonel's daily presentation, I'd view the back end of the cartoon show, presided over by Sheriff Bob, the usual staff announcer doubling as the kiddie host. Sheriff Bob held a weekly contest to generate viewer mail. Send in a postcard with the correct answer to the question of the week, and you'd have a shot at winning a brand-new bike. The questions were pathetic, and in entering, I knew that I, a member of Colonel McCoy's seminar, was unfairly competing with younger and weaker kids. But I sent in my entry regularly, just the same. And won with the successful completion of the line "Little boy blue, come blow your ———!"

Sheriff Bob read out my name, I experienced a moment of unreality, and in a week or so it came, a big carton containing a Schwinn bicycle of beautiful red, unassembled.

My father, whose prowess as a no-hands rider smoking cigarettes whilst pedaling in the Krasinski was

known to us, declared he would put the thing together and demanded he be left completely alone in the
garage for a few minutes. Many minutes passed. Hours
passed. Then, from a window, I saw him making a
number of trips to the car with parts of the bicycle in his
hands. He drove away.

Later: "Tomorrow go to deh bicycle shop. Here's
deh ticket. I remembered I didn't hev it a pump to pump
up deh tires, so I took it dere, deh whole ting—let him
put it togedder, deh bicycle guy. Go, in deh afternoon
vill be raddy."

After getting off the school bus the next day, I
walked three blocks to the bicycle shop and collected
my Schwinn. I had no idea how to ride a bike. The man
in the shop came out onto the pavement and spent a
few minutes getting me started. During my wobbly
progress home, I fell off a number of times, getting my
uniform dirty, and was bruised and sweaty and still far
from in control of the machine when I came upon the
neighborhood kids, who mounted gracefully and rode
out of sight the moment I came into view, as I knew
they would.

I practiced every day, cutting Colonel McCoy's class
to work on my technique. In slow increments, I got
slightly better at riding the thing, and while im-
proving, I increased the pressure in my campaign to
get a dog. I remind the reader that the idea was to
have a dog who'd lope alongside the bike like those of
the neighborhood kids, who always looked like a

Norman Rockwell cover. What kind of a dog need this be? I had no preference. I do, and I did, like all dogs. And yet . . . if I had to pick a single breed of dog, the existence of which I would be hard put to think up an excuse for . . . if I had to pick one breed with no conceivable purpose on earth other than to demonstrate the folly of Man in the person of dog breeders . . . if I had to pick a breed of dog with which I'd rather consort with less than parrots, I'd pick the Boston terrier.

The Boston terrier was originally a cross between a bulldog and a bullterrier, created by a subspecies of human that takes pleasure in organizing dog fights. It is a flat-faced, bug-eyed, wheezing, snorting, snoring, flatulent little excrescence, virtually always delivered by cesarean section because of its ugly oversize knob of a head.

I hardly need tell the reader that it was a Boston terrier my father gave me back in my boyhood bicycle days in Los Angeles.

I remember suggesting a collie or a husky in conversation with my father, which prompted him to begin scouring the classifieds and circling ads for Pomeranians, papillons, and Japanese spaniels. It's no trick for a grown man to coerce a ten-year-old boy in the matter of the choice of a dog. All puppies are cute, and compared with the caprices and grotesques my father usually favored, the Boston terrier appeared a very serviceable sort of dog.

He had located various dealers in dogflesh all in out-of-the-way locations with prisonlike back rooms in which puppies were arrayed in cages. We both had misgivings about Bootsie. Mine were the obvious ones. His, I believe, had to do with the fear that she might not grow up to be sufficiently outlandish and repulsive.

My father need not have worried—what Bootsie lacked in the way of deformity and hideousness (not much, really) would be more than made up for by her quirks of personality.

Bootsie made a good deal of noise when sleeping. She had a delicate stomach, and my mother had to cook special food for her—sheep hearts and kidneys . . . stewed. This was prescribed, and the organs supplied, by my father's animal medical adviser, an unqualified vet who ran a combination clinic and butcher shop and had sold us the dog in the first place.

That Bootsie was an embarrassment around the neighborhood is, of course, an understatement. The image of the loyal dog bounding along beside the bike evaporated before very long. Bootsie was not the bounding sort, let alone loyal. In no time, reality set in. Already I was an outsize kid, similar to a blimp in shape. A nervous, wheezing little dog, looking like a trained flea at the end of her leash, was all I needed to emphasize my awkwardness, and my attempt to convince passersby that I was walking her for someone else only served to mark me as a feebleminded boy who talked to himself.

Bootsie was terrified of my father and wet the carpet whenever he spoke to her. And although she allowed me to leash her up and drag her outdoors, where she found nothing of interest, she never indicated in any way that she recognized me from encounter to encounter. She spent most of her time in the kitchen sitting motionless, her little gargoyle face and bat ears directed toward the gas range, where, come four o'clock, my mother would stew Bootsie's offal.

Even in those days, it had dawned on me that we were not a lovable family, but dogs are supposed to love you even if you're not. Although we'd had Bootsie since her puppyhood, she simply failed to take a liking to any of us. I know this from a hundred signs, but principally because she would leave home every chance she got.

She'd burrow under the fence—two or three days would pass, and we'd get a call from miles away. Someone would have found Bootsie and read our phone number off her collar.

My mother didn't drive, so Bootsie would usually come home in the backseat of a taxi. She'd hang around for a couple of weeks and then run off again. One day she left and never came back. And in a year or two the redolence of sheep kidneys faded enough that visitors ceased to comment on it.

Chapter 6

Nelly, the last dog of my childhood, arrived in a crate, airfreight from Brooklyn. I was home from school, feigning some illness and fooling with the shortwave radio. By this time my parents had moved into their dream house, a sprawling single-story painted a quite vivid pink. It was a famous house insofar as various hot-rod magazines would ask permission to shoot their covers on our crescent driveway. The facade of the house made a perfect background for a 1936 chopped and channeled Chevy in metallic purple with chrome side-mounted exhaust pipes.

My mother was doing some light vacuuming—her housecleaning outfit included high heels, I remember—when the dog was delivered. We opened the crate on the patio, and Nelly stumbled out blinking, nipped me on the hand, drank some water, and wandered off to relieve herself.

"Your uncle Boris is behind this," my mother said. Who else would it have been?

Uncle Boris had decided he was getting too old to

keep a dog, or that the dog needed to live in a house with a yard in California, or maybe it was someone else's dog and he was doing them a favor—all that was sure was that it was consistent with his lifelong practice of sending unwanted gifts.

Nelly was a medium-size mongrel, shaggy and two-toned. She appeared to have been born to be a boy's pal and lope alongside the bike. However, having been raised by a cranky old Jewish man, she instantly attached herself to my father. She pretty much ignored me completely, except to snap when I came near her.

On that first day, my mother clicked around the patio on her high-heeled vacuuming slippers, offering Nelly tidbits, and Nelly wandered here and there, looking around, complacently. When my father came home, she licked the back of his hand once or twice and settled down to snooze nearby.

Nelly was with us for a long time, during which I was effectively blocked from getting a dog of my own. The parental argument was "A dog of your own? You never spend any time with the dog we've already got!"

* * *

I said good-bye to the military school and found myself enrolled in a civilian junior high, where I fell in with a bunch of boy magicians. I became one too. Every Wednesday night, I attended the Magician's Club at the West Side Jewish Community Center, and every Saturday, I squandered my allowance at Joe Berg's Studio of Magic upstairs on Hollywood Boulevard.

On the discount bookshelf at Joe Berg's, I found a copy of a book about hypnosis and invested half a dollar. My idea was to learn to hypnotize and thus acquire a potential encore, or emergency extender, for my magic act. I studied the book and developed considerable proficiency. For the next three or four weeks, I spent lunchtime at school putting my little friends into trances. They seemed to enjoy it. I was never sure whether they were really hypnotized—they would have imitated chickens and so forth under the influence or not—but I was pretty sure I had the technique down pat.

Besides, the real proof was my much older half brother Jack, who visited us often in those days. Jack was the best subject ever born. I could send him into catatonia with the point of a finger. Then I'd give him posthypnotic suggestions: the pencil too heavy to lift, the coin handed to him that he would perceive as red-hot—and his chicken imitation showed real conviction. It got so he'd run out of the house the moment he saw me.

The last chapter of the book dealt with self-hypnosis. It said that no one could call himself a real hypnotist unless he was able to self-hypnotize, and it further said that the only way to learn self-hypnosis was to have a fully qualified hypnotist put you under and teach you. Of course, the author's address was printed in the back of the book in case any student should need additional help—for a modest fee.

It turned out that the author's hypnotic premises

were in a cheap furnished-apartment building located between my house and Joe Berg's Studio of Magic. The hypnotist also had something to do with publishing country and western music, and took orders for rubber stamps. He was a thin guy who wore a Clark Gable mustache and cowboy clothes.

He was courteous and grave. Looking back, I suspect he was three-quarters blotto—but like a good author, he treated a reader of his book with respect. He told me he could teach me self-hypnosis, but since I was a minor, he'd need a note declaring parental permission.

So I asked my father. We were at my sister Elaine's house, and her husband happened to be a physician. My father asked my brother-in-law, "Vhat you tink? Should little Sonnyeh here loin he should put himself into a trence?"

"Better have him checked out by a psychiatrist first," my brother-in-law said. "Make sure he isn't crazy or anything."

Ask a doctor a question, he'll send you to a specialist. So off I was sent to a headshrinker—a lady one—a Viennese one. "Und vhy do you vant to learn to hypnotize yourself?" she asked me.

"Well, it says in the book that in order to be a real hypnotist, you have to know how to hypnotize yourself, and you have to go to a hypnotist to learn that."

"You know, Freud abandoned zuh use of hypnosis after a vhile."

"I beg your pardon?"

"Neffer mind. Ve vill find out zuh real reason. First I vill send you for tests."

"Tests?"

For three days I was excused from school. I went to the children's hospital and had a variety of entertaining tests and interviews with all sorts of doctors. They were all very nice to me. I also ate in the hospital cafeteria and, in general, had a good time.

When I returned to school, my teachers were also extra nice to me. They were concerned because I had been pulled out of school to have psychiatric tests. Several teachers took me aside and asked how I was feeling, and told me that if there was anything in the school routine that I didn't like—that caused me stress—I wouldn't have to do it. This information was not wasted on me.

The psychiatrist told me that I was an intelligent child, and that I probably had many problems that we would discover as time went on. I was to see her every week—which meant leaving school early to take the bus to her office, and being given money so I could eat my supper in a restaurant. She also loaned me a book of stories about the childhoods of famous composers.

When I asked her, she said that she would advise my father not to sign the note allowing me to learn self-hypnosis because it would interfere with my therapy.

I didn't mind, really. I was already getting bored with hypnotism, and even with being a boy magician. And I had discovered what I really wanted to be. A neurotic.

Chapter 7

Now I heroically, and generously, skip my whole adolescence and early adulthood and introduce myself a healthy idiot in my mid-twenties. I pause a moment to savor the gratification of readers who have just realized they won't be subjected to my early disappointments and insights and sexual coming-of-age. Moment over. Thank you. I hope it was as good for you as it was for me.

My father died when I was a senior at Bard, a progressive liberal arts college that, for me, was a four-year rest cure or country vacation where I majored in fresh air and wholesome food. I wound up inheriting the perfect sum of thirty-eight thousand dollars. It was a perfect sum because it wasn't so much that one would have been obliged to think about preserving it, look into investments, never touch capital, and so forth. And it wasn't so much that my rapacious half brother would try to take it away from me. It was the perfect sum to do something with. Friends of mine were heading to graduate school, which struck me as cruel and unusual. I decided to use up the thirty-eight grand, make it last while I finished educating myself. I made it last five years and got two trips to Africa and a station wagon out of it.

Still a healthy idiot in my mid-twenties . . . I moved to Hoboken, which was cheaper than Manhattan—just across the Hudson—where I pursued a career in fine art, for which I had no discernable talent. This does not mean I did not love it and appreciate it. I was just like thousands of my fellow customers at David Davis Fine Art Supplies who were also no good, and more or less knew it, but kept scratching and dabbing because it was so completely engaging and interesting. I had schlepped my stuff to every single gallery and museum in the city, and what I was told was unanimous. I was destined to fail, couldn't do otherwise. This news had a liberating rather than depressing effect. I could devote myself full-time to the study and practice of Art, and the inheritance made my days full of ease and bliss. It was as though I had received a Prix de Rome, or one of those grants, only New York City is better than Rome, and a grant has the potential of making one think one has some kind of talent, and maybe an obligation. This was tourism at home, retirement while young. I was in a good mood all the time.

I worked in my studio all day just as though anybody cared, visited museums and galleries regularly, consorted with other artists I had met at David Davis's, had a series of girlfriends of the sort who might be expected to pair up with a lousy artist—in other words, great-looking and stupid—and occasionally threw parties for my bohemian friends.

On two or three occasions I sold a picture, and I once had my work included in a group show at the Brooklyn Museum—just enough recognition to provide credentials, which got me some jobs teaching art classes in settlement houses.

I had a cat, Zoe, who came from one of the very Manhattan pet shops where my father had sought tiny monkeys when I was a tiny boy. Cage-bound for too long at the pet shop, unsocialized, plain stupid, she was so limited she never left the floor. Jumping up onto a chair was beyond her gifts. A Maine coon, she was long-legged and had arresting eyes and was, in most respects, like any of my girlfriends of the period.

I knew I would use up my subsidy one day. I had a long-range plan in the event that I wasn't able to locate a means of survival in the art world. One option was to get a job with the post office, traditional haven for dreamers and intellectuals. I'd be like Melville working in the customhouse, only I would be a cheerful postal worker, unlike Herman, who was bugged because his career as a writer had tanked. I had already taken the exam, and my route carrier had spotted me as having the right stuff, and encouraged me, and let me know he and his colleagues would welcome my company.

My preferred choice, which might have been a better choice for Herman too, was to be a deckhand on the Erie Lackawanna ferries. These were graceful, steam-powered boats, built in the middle of the nineteenth century by the Stevens brothers, who had instituted the first regular ferry service in the country. Delicate of line, fitted out with towering smokestacks, mahogany staircases, mirrors that had reflected nearly a hundred years of voyagers and commuters, and magnificent shining brass engines—smooth, quiet, and powerful— the boats surged out into the central channel, then downriver, and turned in to the slips at Barclay Street, lower Manhattan. The trip cost a quarter and took a little more than twenty minutes.

Equipped with a couple of much-better-than-average hot dogs purchased in the Erie Lackawanna Railroad station on the Hoboken side, I'd lunch on board nearly every fine day. Sometimes I'd make an extra couple of crossings to enjoy the New York skyline and the pleasure of being on the water. One didn't pay another fare if one stayed on board, and I passed many a bright afternoon crossing the river again and again, reading, gazing, and dozing. I memorized the duties of the deckhands, which included opening and closing the gates at either end of the boat, tossing a rope line, and wielding a mop. I applied for the job and inquired at the office once a week for three years, hoping there would be a vacancy and knowing full well that anyone giving up such a job would have to be crazy.

The ferries and their predecessors had made the crossing since 1811. Lafayette had ridden one. Napoléon III had ridden one, Stephen Foster, Frank Sinatra, Willem de Kooning, Allen Ginsberg, me! Holidaymakers in the early nineteenth century had taken the ferry to the parks and amusements of Hoboken. The first organized baseball game was played in Hoboken, and the spectators arrived by water. Thousands of people had commuted from suburban New Jersey to jobs on Wall Street. Others had begun or ended cross-country rail journeys with a Hoboken ferry ride. When the rest of the United States had prohibition, Hoboken simply didn't, and the ferries ran all night.

When it was announced in 1967 that the service was going to be discontinued on November 22, a lot of people reflected and remembered. I rode the ferry every day during its last week, taking pictures and storing up memories. The final crossing was at nightfall. Underused in recent years, the boat was packed now. Bands were playing on the upper and lower decks, champagne flowed. The crew invited passengers down to see the engine, shiny as the day it was made, effortlessly propelling the boat through the black water.

Every light was burning, and all the other river traffic was lit up. Horns sounded. Bells rang. The fireboats projected great streams of water into the air. Red distress flares were discharged. Some people cried. We sang "Auld Lang Syne" as we pulled into the slip in Hoboken.

The boat thumped to a final stop. There was a long moment. Silence. And then the crowd began to trash the boat. I saw seats pried up, newel posts rocked free, and every one of the orange cork-filled life jackets left the boat in the hands of a sentimental passenger. I saw a tiny middle-aged woman attempting to carry one of the ship's wheels down the gangway.

It was a human moment, and particularly a Hoboken moment. I don't know that I thought it then, but that night marks for me the beginning of my realization that my days as a postgraduate beatnik were coming to an end.

Chapter 8

The Glade and Glen Boys' Farm was once a poor-farm, county insane asylum, and orphanage. Toward the end of the nineteenth century, wealthy suburbs with splendid estates had grown up around it, and the place became a blight on the neighborhood. Unable to get rid of it, some of the local gentry subscribed to a fund for prettying up the place. The effect was picturesque to a stunning degree. Adorable half-timbered cottages with fake thatched roofs, split-rail fences, and shady lanes were created. It looked like a movie set—part Boy's Town, part prep school. There was a working farm, a pond jumping with sunfish and crawdads, playing fields, and a friendly low-slung main building, looking like the clubhouse at an exclusive old country club.

I had an interview for a job as art teacher. It was early fall, and the place looked like Technicolor. I wouldn't have been surprised to see Roddy McDowall or Elizabeth Taylor ride up on a thoroughbred. I met with the headmistress of the Glade and Glen Boys' Farm Residential School. Ms. Susie Spinner was the daughter of a former headmaster, and completely and obviously demented. Her eyes darted around the room as she spoke—she interrupted herself, lapsed into reminiscence about her childhood, and giggled girlishly apropos of nothing. Every few minutes she asked me my name, and three times she asked me why I was there. It occured to me that this might be some kind of test to see whether 1) I was at ease with and kind to mentally disturbed persons, or 2) whether I would notice she was seriously loony and mention it to another member of the staff.

However, at the end of the interview, she told me I had the job, and I decided to overlook the fact that she was still talking to someone invisible when I left her office.

Ms. Spinner had told me the school had a clientele of boys between eight and eleven years of age. They included mildly disturbed, mildly retarded, and mildly antisocial individuals—nothing hard-core. Most of the boys came from good families in the suburbs of New York City and were expected to go on to respected boarding schools and then Ivy League colleges.

I didn't exactly believe her. I had gone to a school along similar lines myself. The very next day, I set about tidying up the art room, making an inventory of supplies, and listing things I would need. I'd been attending a seminar given by art therapist Lucile Potts, and I was full of techniques and ideas that would be just right for the mildly mixed-up kids at Glade and Glen.

Five or six young men appeared at the door of my art room. They were in their early twenties or the end of their teens, had beards, and were notably burly, with massive shoulders and bulging upper arms. They were dressed in overalls and yellow work boots, neckerchiefs, baseball caps. I thought maybe they had come to move furniture.

"Yes? Can I help you?" I asked them.

"I doubt it," one of the men said. "You're supposed to show us how to do art or something."

"I am?"

"We're your nine o'clock class," one of them said.

"You're . . . students here?"

"Well, mostly we work on the farm. We live here."

"Been here long?"

"Twelve . . . fifteen years. Ms. Spinner said to come here and do art."

"How old are you guys?"

"Twenty, twenty-one . . . Fred is twenty-three."

"Only we don't want to do art."

"What do you want to do?"

"Well, we were thinking of messing you up."

"What's your next choice?"

"I dunno. Sit down and rest. Have a smoke."

"Take chairs, gentlemen. Light up. Consider this room your private club until ten o'clock. As of the next time you are scheduled to come here, I will have a full pack for your pleasure."

"We don't like filter tips."

"Of course not."

"And we don't mess you up, right?"

"Right."

The *Of Mice and Men* crowd came only once a week. They had all been at Glade and Glen since they were quite small. I don't think they remembered anything before being there. I didn't push the art thing. I let them sit and smoke, and they refrained from tearing me limb from limb. The little gang of lifers didn't exhibit any particular pathology, as far as I could tell. They were on the slow side, but I suspect all that was wrong with them was that they had been institutionalized almost all their lives.

The younger, I should say actual, kids tended to be livelier, wilder, twitchier, sicker. They were a completely mixed bag of disturbed, delinquent, deficient, and merely unwanted. What they had in common was that they had gotten lost in the system.

I came to know my colleagues on the faculty. They were something of a mirror image of the kids. Each of them had a past they didn't want to talk about. There were plenty of quirks and idiosyncracies, and I soon began to suspect that my own qualifications for being there, while barely good enough, were lots better than anyone else's.

There was a school shrink who was present one half-day per week, worked in the office, and didn't see any kids. He was tall, stooped, and had a Vandyke beard. When he walked by the open door of the art room one day, the kids registered real fear. They clustered around me. "That's . . . that's the headshrinker! Don't go near him . . . he'll shrink your head."

Given the variety and degree of problems, there should have been two adults to a class, but there was only one. We were strictly forbidden to leave the kids alone. If a teacher needed to use the bathroom, or get a smoke to calm his nerves, he had to march his whole class to another classroom, where the teacher on duty would watch both bunches. Of course, relative pandemonium would ensue, and there was no hope of getting the kids calmed down and doing their lesson, or doing art, once the groups had been separated.

The kids themselves knew how to make use of the never-left-alone rule. If an individual kid got up and walked out of the classroom, the teacher could either shoo the other kids into a neighboring classroom or drag them along and follow the kid who had walked, entreating him to return to the room.

Some kids also had fits, seizures, and episodes, as well as fistfights, hysterics, and shaking terror, all of which were apt to trigger the other kids into their particular behaviors.

There was only one way to preserve peace and have a faint hope of doing anything constructive. That was to bribe or coax one of the three mongrel dogs who ranged over the campus to hang out in one's classroom. When a dog was present, the kids were usually able to control themselves—and influence one another. A kid would begin to go into whatever characteristic acting-out his illness required of him, and another kid would hush him. "Be quiet! You'll upset the dog."

I began to fill my pockets with scraps and treats for the four-legged brutes, in addition to cigarettes for the human ones. And I began to fantasize about having a dog of my own, a special, kind, and patient dog who'd come to work with me and heal these kids.

Chapter 9

I was driving in Manhattan on a rainy night. Just for a few seconds, in the periphery of my headlights, I caught sight of two extraordinary dogs between parked cars. They were large, wolflike, but also highly decorative in a barbaric way, with strong symmetrical markings. They seemed graceful, and somehow, in that fleeting glimpse, I got the impression they had an intelligent look in their eyes.

I sort of knew what they were—sled dogs of some kind. But my image of huskies until now had been of smaller, scruffier, and less colorful dogs, desperate ruffians I had seen in films, yipping noisily and pulling a sled. These were aristocratic and clean of limb. I was impressed. I was more than impressed. I was smitten. This was the sort of dog I wanted to live with.

The image of the two dogs stayed with me, vivid and alive. I wanted to see them again.

I got two paperback books at a pet shop. One was

All About Siberian Huskies, and the other *All About Alaskan Malamutes.* Published by the same outfit, the books appeared to have identical texts, with the name of the breed changed. They had different photographs.

What text there was ran to the effect that the noble sled dogs of the North were trustworthy, loyal, helpful, friendly, courteous, kind, obedient, cheerful, thrifty, brave, clean, and reverent; had saved many children from burning houses; and could easily be taught to carry messages and cash checks for their owners. The pictures showed various champion show dogs looking glamorous. And I had another book about dogs.

Lorenz, du bist ein dummkopf! Good writer, though. Now that I've been an author myself for years and years, I can see how it happened. Then, I didn't know.

There was a book twenty-some years ago that told all about how ribonucleic acid would reverse the aging process. Sardines, said the distinguished scientist author, were the foodstuff most rich in RNA. For a summer, you couldn't find a tin of sardines on the Upper East Side of New York, and grocers were charging double.

How did this scientific miracle get published, and why aren't we all full of sardines and playing volleyball on the beach to this very day? Well, the editor at the publishing house read the manuscript, then went home and ate sardines three times a day for three weeks. When she looked in the mirror, damn if a lot of her wrinkles hadn't gone away. A contract was written, the book was published, it was a best-seller, lots of sardines got eaten, the editor got sick of eating sardines, stopped eating sardines and thus reduced her elevated intake of salt, ceased retaining so much water, lost the facial puffiness, and the wrinkles came back.

Closer to home, one day my wife and I sat in the office of a book editor and pitched the idea of a book about choosing, raising, and training a puppy. The editor liked the idea and offered us a contract, which we accepted. As it happened, we knew what we were talking about, but at no time did he, or anyone else connected with the publication of the book, ask us why we thought we were qualified to write such a thing. We never even mentioned that we owned or had ever owned a dog.

When I read *Man Meets Dog*, I had no way of knowing that the caraway seeds in Konrad Lorenz's sauerkraut had fermented and addled his brain. He put forth a theory that there are two races of dog: Der Dogg, und Der Uberdogg. No kidding—he said there are dogs descended from jackals (*Canis aureus*), and dogs descended from wolves (*Canis lupus*). The jackal types are, well, doglike—they're fawning, curry favor with their masters, are perpetually juvenile and subservient, and . . . not that we don't love them and wish them no harm . . . they're secretive, clannish, extra clever, and good with money. Whereas wolf-descended dogs . . . well, they are a whole other matter—they are noble and decent, and dignified, and heroic, and call no man master who has not shown that he too has Aryan virtues. Some of them even have blue eyes.

Of course Konrad didn't put it like that. They never do. And the dear old fellow surely would have been horrified to hear me say he was full of bratwurst, and a racist. They always are. If he'd actually done any science, like comparing skeletons and gross physical characteristics, he'd have observed that all dogs, jackals included, descend from the ancestral wolf, and wolves are simply wild dogs—they can interbreed with domestic dogs, they have only trifling physical differences—and if Konrad had ever lived with a wolf, or a dog with strong wolf traits, he would have noticed that the ratio of dignified and heroic to downright silly is something like one to twenty. Standard for all dogs . . . and humans.

Lorenz theorized that one would create the best of dogs by blending the wolf type, say a chow chow, with a jackal type, say a German shepherd; then one would have the perfect combination of independence and subservience. This just happened to be the very brand of mutt Konrad himself owned. What he had observed was that chow chows (which are in fact descended from something like a wolf) are quite stubborn and difficult, and German shepherds (which are in fact descended from something like a wolf) are trainable and cooperative—and when he bred the two together, he got some dogs he liked . . . because they were his dogs.

Naturally, I fell for the whole romance, only I was sure that I wanted to have a pure experience with a pure wolf-descended dog. This inclination was related to the fact that men, no matter how ridiculous their physique, will stand in front of a mirror flexing their muscles. I saw myself as some kind of Nordic or Eskimo Jewish barbarian, clad in furs and foot rags, with my noble wolf by my side.

Sled dogs look like wolves. They like to pose for pictures standing on some rock, gazing into the distance, looking like Siegfried. What they are thinking at such a moment, when the last rays of the sun are hitting their grizzled and handsome coats, and their intelligent profiles are to be seen at their best, is probably: "Soon I will move my bowels. Yes. That is what I will do." Or, "If I pee on this rock, other dogs will come and smell it, and know I was here."

This reality was unknown to me. The dogs of my childhood had mostly ignored me, and I had learned nothing by observing them. In fact, I had no idea where I got the notion one could interact with a dog, or that there would be any reason to want to. I was limited to my fantasies and what I could learn from reading. I kept the two picture books and the Konrad Lorenz book by my bedside and looked at them every night before going to sleep.

Chapter 10

I was driving in Manhattan on another rainy night. Just for a few seconds, in the periphery of my headlights, I caught sight of an extraordinary woman between parked cars. She had astonishing red hair, was graceful and lithe, and her expression was a mixture of sweetness and intelligence.

This was right in the middle of my Brigham Young, or *this-is-it!,* period. I was making life decisions at the drop of a hat. It's not that I was reckless or didn't care. I had come to a certain understanding through my study of Zen Buddhism, and observation, particularly in connection with my activity as an artist. What I understood was this: It's possible for an educated person to deny the evidence of his own eyes and think he's seeing something else based on whatever prejudices he's been taught. We know what we're doing at all times—and at almost all times, we obscure that knowledge with thought. So, I reasoned, having barely had a look at her, there was no real reason not to decide a particular woman was the person one wanted to spend the rest of one's life with. According to my belief at the time, only distraction brought on by inappropriate mentation or corrupt doctrine could result in a wrong decision.

Jill wasn't as wordy about it as I tend to be, but apparently she believed what amounted to the same thing. We were married six weeks after we first met. That was more than thirty years ago—and for almost all of those years we've worked at home, as writers and artists, so we've been in each other's company close to 100 percent of the time.

Notwithstanding that the marriage showed signs of working out from the first, I lost confidence in the accuracy of my instant intuition a year later after I bought a French Citroën car. But that's another story. While my confidence in my own snap judgments was still intact, we courted, married, moved Jill out of a once-in-a-lifetime Manhattan apartment and into my creaky Hoboken loft.

This included cats. Jill had two. I had one . . . remember Zoe, the animated dust mop? Zoe and Jill's two cats did not get along. We hadn't bothered to introduce them before combining households. We had assumed they'd work something out. Besides, the idea of reconsidering a marriage because our pets didn't like one another was too idiotic—not that we weren't idiots. But here we were, married, and the cats would not settle down.

We decided the fair thing would be to find homes for the lot of them and start over. I got a first look at Jill's energy and powers of organization. It's not easy placing an adult cat, let alone three, but she did it. Then we were catless. Winter had set in. We had planned a belated honeymoon to take place during the Christmas school vacation (Jill was teaching at a university). Everything was in readiness, our tickets bought, reservations made, and most of our cash converted to traveler's checks. Then, just before we were to set out for Paris . . . we caught the flu.

It wasn't the usual flu. It was the mother of all flus. We were devastated. The trip was impossible. We spent what would have been our first few days in Paris in our Hoboken loft, bundled up, eating soup, sniffling, whimpering. And there were no cats! Cats are essential when you are confined with an illness. Even Zoe, who had the intellect of an amoeba, could at least hunker nearby and purr. Jill's cats would have shared body warmth and comforted us—but they were beginning new relationships, giving aid and succor to other flu victims, not us.

Jill found this particularly bitter and, at her lowest, cursed the day she had met me and given up Thor and Tyche for a mere husband. I, swathed in quilts and racked with fever, conceived a wild plan to cheer her and get back in her good graces. I thrust the paperback books about huskies and Malamutes her way and, for good measure, a book about domestic cats.

We had all that honeymoon money, all those traveler's checks. When we were well enough to get around town, our first stop was at an overpriced cattery on the East Side.

For a sum equivalent to a little less than three months' rent, we took title to a sweet little Abyssinian kitten. We named her Sadie. Sadie came with a long list of dos and don'ts, a boxful of cattery-approved equipment and toys, and a long-playing record that told us how to take care of our cat.

She was a joy, and went a long way toward completing our healing. Jill bonded with the little kitten. As an Abyssinian, Sadie was energetic and athletic, and the special diet of home-cooked cat food prescribed by the cattery gave her even more vigor and a degree and power of flatulence that was nothing short of astounding.

But this was only the first phase. There were traveler's checks remaining, and I had something more planned.

Chapter *11*

It has to be understood that I learned just about nothing from the dogs of my childhood. Most of what I knew about dogs came out of those two paperbacks, and of course there was Konrad. It seems he later retracted the whole theory, said he had been drinking a lot of Kirschwasser and listening to his Wagner records the night he cooked it up.

But this news came too late for me. I was still intent on getting something large, primitive, and built for sled hauling, and I had talked Jill into it too. So it happened that on a winter's day, we drove upstate in search of Gussik Kennels, where the purest and finest Alaskan Malamutes were bred—so said the brochure.

As we crunched across the snow, approaching the modest house, we heard a sound one never forgets. Fifteen or twenty Malamutes in the kennel behind the house raised their voices in a sustained howl. The hair on the back of my neck stood up. It was powerful. It was primal. It was scary.

A little shaky in the knees, we continued trudging and met Franz Gussik, the dog breeder. Here was a classic slob, taller and fatter than me, with a three-day growth of beard, wearing greasy thermal long johns, overalls, and insulated boots. He had an openmouthed, gaping, staring expression and drooled slightly. He stood listing to the left or right and looked at us with his head cocked to the side. He breathed loudly and scratched himself with dirt-encrusted fingernails. I had no basis for comparison at the time, but I now know that as dog breeders go, he was above average. He could read and write, and I believe had never eaten a child of his own.

I don't know that, since then, I have ever heard a bunch of Malamutes spontaneously howl a greeting, or warning, to signal someone's approach. Conceivably there might be some yelping and vocalizing, but a group howl isn't likely. All he'd have to do is look out the window, see a couple of prospective customers coming, and give out with a howl himself. The dogs would take it up, and the visitors would reach the house in an excited and impressionable state of mind.

This is certainly what Franz Gussik must have done. Brutish-looking though he was, we were putty in his hands from the moment we shook his meaty paw. He launched at once into flattering me by treating me as if I were an expert. This is devastating when working on a man in the presence of a woman. As I said, I knew practically nothing, and it was likely that Jill knew I knew practically nothing—but Franz Gussik wasn't going to allow me to think about anything. Instead, he solicited my opinion about this and that and peppered me with jargon.

"This one's dam went best of opposite bitch reserve at the Grand National Bahamian Specialty," he would say, thrusting a cute, squirming ball of fur at me. "Oh, I can see you're a superior judge of dogflesh. Never mind that batch of pups over there—a failed experiment, slunky hocks—but look who I'm telling about slunky hocks. I saw you notice their fettles were undershot before I said a word."

While Franz Gussik was speaking, his wife and daughters brought armload after armload of puppies into the small living room. Three dozen pups of all sizes were scampering around, not to mention two or three adult nursing mothers.

Up close the dogs seemed huge. I was a little afraid of them. Franz Gussik spoke incessantly, describing the virtues and drawbacks of various puppies. Not only did I not understand anything he was saying, I couldn't tell which puppy he was talking about.

"Now let me explain about breeder's terms," he was saying. "This little lady is Gussik's Song of Bernadette (my wife's favorite movie). Should you wish to purchase this pup, you have to promise to breed her at least twice and give me the first and third pick of each litter. Any other pups I can sell for you on commission, and you'll realize a handsome profit. If you agree to breed her four times, I will waive the stud fee and pay for all the puppies' shots."

Gussik was trying to involve us in a pyramid scheme. He did with dogs like others do with vitamins and home-cleaning products. At one point he was explaining how he could set me up with a complete kennel, and how I could recruit others for the Gussik system.

Meanwhile, Jill was sitting on the floor, fooling with the only puppy in the place who looked sick. It was slow-moving and listless, its coat was coarse, and its eyes were dull. It was coughing. She was cuddling it. In a matter of moments she'd bond with the little pathetnoid. Then it would be months of medical crises, vet bills, then agony and death.

I had to act fast. A puppy, larger than any of the others, had just been let in. It bounded around the room, knocking over every other pup. This pup was mostly black, with a look of hilarious devilry in its eyes.

"I've made up my mind!" I shouted. "I want to buy that puppy!"

"Never!" Franz Gussik shouted back. "You are pointing at Gussik's Abishag. That pup I picked out for myself! She has astonishing potential. I expect to achieve fame and greatness with this animal. She's not for sale, and that's final."

"How much?" I asked him.

"Five hundred dollars."

"I'll give you four-fifty and you'll never see me again."

"Done!"

That was how we acquired Gussik's Abishag, whom we never called anything but Juno. Franz Gussik tried to throw in the sick puppy for an extra fifty, but I outstepped him. While he was distracted with counting cash, I hustled Jill and Juno out to the car.

Chapter 12

Franz Gussik had given us elaborate instructions on the care of our puppy. The first one was, never take her to a vet. Instead, we were to bring her back to Gussik. He would administer what shots she needed and advise us about health matters. He was full of wisdom. "Tapeworm," he said, "is hereditary. All dogs have it." In the words of the veterinarian we took Juno to see the very next day, "All breeders think they would have made great vets if they'd only been able to finish high school."

Born in a snowdrift, the little Malamute gasped and panted and could sleep comfortably only in front of an open window—which meant we had to bundle up considerably.

Sadie, the Abyssinian kitten, and Juno struck an understanding immediately. The loft apartment was eighty-eight feet long, which gave them ample distance for building up speed, and they would actually push off the walls, a couple of feet above the floor, as they took corners. In addition to running laps at remarkable velocity, Juno would chew to bits personal possessions—my Dunhill pipe, my Ultraflex fountain pen, my Icelandic woolen socks—that the cat would knock off shelves for her.

As Juno progressed though puppyhood, passing from what would correspond with infancy to childhood and adolescence, we saw her personality take shape, a combination of traits denoting her membership in the Order of Carnivores, the family Canidae, genus Canis, domestic in species (only just), and of the ancient breed that has served man in North America for ten thousand years. Add to these qualities that she was a M'Loot, descended from dogs only lately discovered in the remote interior of Alaska. Where nature and the forces of evolution stopped shaping her particular strain and ancestry, Man took over, beginning with whatever ancient Amerind peoples had selected dogs for the harness against dogs for the pot, and winding up at Gussik Kennels, where a dropout with one of those paperback how-to books did his best to improve the breed.

Juno's essential disposition was in her every molecule and as immutable as her hard bones and ivory teeth. Being a dog, she came equipped with more specific knowledge than she would acquire in her lifetime, and the strongest directive of her whole heredity was to ascend as far as she could in the hierarchy of the wolf pack. Dogs are yuppies. They have the corporate mentality. They will climb up your body to get to the top. This is all dogs. Malamutes are more so. I am not suggesting that there was anything vicious about Juno. She simply assigned ranks to everyone in her family and periodically tried to improve hers. This is essential for efficiency and survival in the wild. If the head wolf is getting old and weak, or blind, or stupid, somebody had better find out about it and replace him before he gets the whole group into trouble.

Dogs, or wolves, are not necessarily unhappy if they can't be number one. Dogs like to know where they belong, and in group or pack situations, they will settle contentedly for the role they are dealt. Except some dogs. Some dogs will never stop challenging. It's encoded. They're dominant. Put them in their place and they'll bide their time—and then challenge the leader again. This challenge is not to be construed as a bared-fangs squaring-off followed by a leap at the throat. It need be only a deliberate act of defiance, such as looking the master right in the eye and pissing on the floor. Fail to do something about it there and then, and the escalation to full-scale insurrection and anarchy will be swift.

Can there be any question that Juno, our little darling furball, was one of those alpha dogs? This is how she viewed our family (her dog pack): number-one wolf—me; number-two wolf—Jill; number-three wolf—Juno herself; and honorary fourth wolf—the cat.

With the cat, all was well. She was small and had to defer to Juno. They were good friends and played continually, but Juno would make an occasional point of shifting Sadie from a comfortable spot just to prove that she had the right.

With me, all was well. I was the undisputed leader, the big male, he with the commanding voice and strong right arm. It was how I saw myself too. Juno generally obeyed me, fawned on me, and flirted with me.

Juno saw Jill as something between a mother and a rival. While she'd come to Jill directly when hurt, and would have sought her protection if she had ever been frightened by anything (which I don't recall happening), she resented having to take orders from her and would obey with that comic slowness that amounts to an insult.

Juno also found opportunities when playing to sneak a little higher up the social ladder. All of us roughhoused a lot, and while Juno knew better than—and had no inclination—to bite flesh, there was no rule against grabbing hold of clothing in the heat of the game and maybe ripping it a little. Jill hardly owned a pair of blue jeans without rents around the cuffs—all of mine were intact. Any time Jill sat on the floor, as she likes to do, Juno was apt to sneak up behind her, grab her by the belt, and drag her out of the room. And on many a night, a Malamute would slide between the sleeping couple and up beneath the covers from the foot of the bed, place her back against me, her four huge feet against Jill, and slowly shove her out of the bed. Mornings when Jill would arise before me, I might wake to the sight of a grotesquely grinning face on the pillow next to mine, gazing lovingly on her sleeping master.

Juno and I spent a good deal of time on our own, walking and hiking. She was built for sustained locomotion and enjoyed covering distances. I like to walk myself, so we made a good team. One particular pleasure was taking Juno out in snowstorms. There were plenty of them during Juno's first winter with us, and it was possible to get lost in a whiteout down the street in the plaza by the Erie Lackawanna Railroad station and the tugboat docks in Hoboken. Juno was a different dog when the snow was falling. She became alert in a way completely different from her usual state of mind. She sniffed the air, tasted the snow, seemed to be taking note of landmarks invisible to me, and was able to shift gears, engaging what amounted to four-wheel drive.

After midnight on the deserted Little League field in the park, I would turn her loose, and she would streak over the open spaces, making a plume of snow behind her, chewing up miles with a long, stretching, powerful gait. Then she might come straight at me, smiling broadly in the sled-dog way, her tongue lolling out hilariously, and bowl me over. We'd tumble and wrestle, colliding again and again, until, exhausted, we'd collapse in the snow, the puppy with her head on my chest, wriggling with happiness, the falling flakes flashing in the light of the streetlamps.

Hiking on trails in state parks revealed yet another side of Juno. She became completely serious and appeared to feel responsible for our welfare and survival. She was able to memorize our route and would insist I return exactly the way I had come. If there was a rock on the trail, for example, and I had passed on the east side of it on our way in, Juno would physically force me to go around the same side on the way back. And if I took her back to the same spot a year later, she would try to get me to pass the rock on the east side again. I believe she never forgot anything she'd seen by way of landmarks, and generally knew where she was at all times.

She was incapable of getting tired. If I stopped to rest on the trail, she would scamper up and down a steep rock face, or practice tightrope walking on a fallen tree—anything but stop moving—all the while shooting me impatient or quizzical looks: "How long are you going to just *sit* there?"

Chapter *13*

Both Jill and I have won prizes for works of literature. We have received honors and plaudits from the great and the wise. We hold degrees from distinguished eastern colleges. We are respected by our friends and feared by our enemies. We have prospered through our enterprise and energy and have done works of charity. I can explain abstruse and difficult points of philosophy, and Jill's advice is sought by everyone.

Only someone who has raised a puppy will appreciate that our proudest boast is this: We are able to housebreak most any healthy dog within a week or ten days. Now, when Juno was a puppy, this, the single greatest secret possessed of mankind, was not known to us.

I am going to impart this secret to the reader. It will not be of interest to everyone, and it interrupts the narrative—but for those to whom it applies, it will be of value beyond measure, and will cause them to bless my name and buy many copies of this very book as gifts for loved ones.

First, the puppy must be of sufficient age to exercise physical control. This varies, but three months is a good rule of thumb. Second, the puppy must be free of intestinal parasites and in otherwise good health. Third, the housebreaker must observe and note the natural pattern of elimination.

Most dogs, if fed on a regular schedule, will eliminate on a regular schedule as well—insofar as solid deposits are concerned. For liquids, this is less true, and one should follow the standard approach of keeping an eye on the pup and whisking it out-of-doors when it begins to circle and sniff meaningfully. Once outdoors, take the puppy to the same specific area and praise it immoderately as it piddles—the same goes for pooping.

Pooping will take place at roughly the same times each day. Let us say that the looked-for event will transpire about twenty minutes after eating. Having established this, take the dog out fifteen minutes after eating.

This is more or less standard so far. Here's our secret: The dog owner will have obtained a jar of glycerin suppositories for infants and children. These are waxy, tapered objects, about the size of a wooden kitchen match. When inserted into the rectum they begin to melt. This causes a sensation—not an irritation—that promotes the moving of bowels, usually within fifteen minutes. Just before taking the dog out, straddle its body facing backward, raise its tail, and insert a suppository. This obviates the well-known experience of walking, and walking, and *walking* the dog until it finally decides to do its business—an especially useful technique at one in the morning in a driving rain. Some few dogs are able to clamp down and resist the action of the suppository or surreptitiously get rid of it. If you haven't seen results after fifteen minutes, simply insert another suppository. Rare is the dog who can resist two, and no dog can resist three. When the puppy delivers, praise it volubly, stroke it, fall to your knees and give thanks to God, gather it to your bosom and kiss it on the mouth, do a happy dance in the street. Then walk the dog around for a few minutes so that it will not associate taking a dump with the end of its pleasant outing.

If you don't miss any scheduled trips outside, given that the puppy has been *made* to eliminate outdoors (and been praised for it), it will be incapable of soiling inside the house and will be on the way to being habituated to saving pooping for out-of-doors. Should it make a mistake or two, it is told "No!" (once!) scornfully, then escorted to its outdoor pooping place, where it is spoken to encouragingly and praised when it produces results. Making a big fuss over indoor mistakes tends to be counterproductive, and rubbing the puppy's nose in its mess only contributes to teaching it to eat stools.

Once the process is fairly started, the owner should introduce a code word of encouragement to be repeated while the puppy is in the act of eliminating. After a week or two, this word will become associated with, and then take the place of, the glycerin suppository. To my dog, I say "Hurry up" and "Lift your leg" for the respective tasks, and he instantly complies—although there is no reason one might not substitute the name of one's employer or ex-spouse, if desired.

With this, I have empowered the reader to obtain the first of the three essential requirements of any pet dog, the other two being not to bite and to walk cooperatively on the leash. Letters of thanks and spontaneous gifts of money (checks only) may be sent to me in care of the publisher.

Chapter 14

I didn't really know why I wanted a dog when I persuaded Jill we needed a Malamute, which didn't take much effort. Jill loves dogs and has always known why. She had a collie when her family moved to the suburbs. Someone had advertised in the classified section that a collie would be given to the child who wrote the best essay. Jill sent one in, then went off to summer camp. While she was there, someone came in the night and tied a collie with health problems to her parents' front doorknob. The family nursed the dog, Penny, and she and Jill spent years together, crashing through such underbrush as had not yet been subdivided.

But I hadn't had that sort of experience. The dogs I'd known in my own childhood had been unsuitable pals, or they hadn't been allowed to stay long enough to establish a relationship, or they simply didn't like me. All that was fueling my dog-owning fantasy—which began when I wished for a canine classroom assistant at Glade and Glen—was Milo's dog-owning fantasy, shared with me in childhood. Of course, he'd dreamed up his particular doggy dream while sitting in the orphanage, waiting for our mother to find a new gangster to look after her and hers, and never had a dog for more than a couple of days until he was in his mid-thirties. (That dog was Chappie-Chan, a Maltese who came along with a house in Tokyo that had snazzy, out-of-date decor, including a faux-leopard couch, a kidney-shaped coffee table, black lacquer Stromberg-Carlson cabinet TV, and an unusually tall and vaguely film-noir Japanese wife. What? Did the reader assume anyone grew up normal in my family? I'm tempted to digress further and tell about the Polish anthropologist who lived in our apartment during World War II, working on a project of national security, and did all the cooking for the family in lieu of rent. To keep her mind on her work, she cooked Japanese dishes exclusively, or anyway a Polish person's idea of Japanese dishes, which may have set Milo's course for the Orient.)

Getting back to my own complete lack of actual experience and utter ignorance about dogs—reasonable expectations to the contrary, things worked out terribly well with Juno. This was not because I did anything right. Housebreaking, which I now find as daunting as going down to the corner for a quart of milk, took weeks and weeks, maybe months. Juno, cooperative as almost every dog, must have interpreted my unclear and inconsistent signals as meaning I wanted to draw the matter out as long as possible and have many hilarious experiences.

The same was true for walking on furniture, destroying property, crawling into the laps of people who were terrified of dogs, and running the Indianapolis 500 with Sadie at three in the morning. And these were merely undesirable behaviors. Where was the bonding and friendship, the affection and unspoken rapport?

They were there right from the beginning. And it wasn't I who kept our whole relationship from being that of a recalcitrant pup and a frustrated, stupid man. It was Juno. She was naturally courteous and friendly. Like most of the dogs I've known, and practically all the dogs of her type, she was anxious that every person feel at ease and comfortable, and she made it clear that she genuinely liked people and enjoyed their company.

Thus, Juno made friends wherever we took her, and she developed a taste for socializing and travel. She was outgoing and friendly to people we met while hiking, but when we went camping in state parks, she'd rise up in the firelight and scare the hell out of anyone who stumbled into our campsite at night.

We had taken a course of private instruction at Captain McInerney's Canine Academy, where I was taught a scheme of obedience training unchanged since the Imperial German Army prior to World War I. Juno took to it, but it was more than she needed and inculcated habits in me that were hard to break later on.

Looking back over Juno's long life, I can remember

her accompanying us to the Williamsburg Inn, the Nassau Inn in Princeton, and riding the steamer to Nantucket (in its day the most dog-friendly place I've ever seen: Juno was welcome on the public bus, the library, and the outdoor or wharfside portion of restaurants). We also took her on a National Park Service launch, where we viewed the spectacle of the wild ponies of Chincoteague Island, Virginia. Not only did Juno obviously enjoy herself on these occasions, she seemed to add to the pleasure of everyone present.

When we first tried taking Juno to a motel, she loved it. Ice from the machine down the hall chilled her water. She intuited that we didn't care if she sprawled on Howard Johnson's bedspread, and there were such interesting smells, not to mention many strangers to meet in the lobby and grounds, brand-new places to poop, air-conditioning. She was a satisfied customer.

That is, as long as we didn't try to economize. Motels with a numeral in their names did not pass muster with Juno. God forbid we should stop someplace with linoleum instead of carpet. Besides the clicking of her toenails as she paced half the night, there were the sighs and mumbling, and the dirty looks and sulking. We learned something more: Some Malamutes have the souls of shop girls.

One single moment comes closest to summing up my friendship with Juno. It's a moment I've experienced many times since, but the first instance I was aware of took place on those cliffs on the west side of the Hudson River. We'd been hiking strenuously and were taking a rest. We were sitting on a rock, looking out over the river toward Yonkers. It was a perfect spring day, brilliant sky, new leaves and grasses, fragrant breezes. We felt good.

After a while, I began to realize that the dog and I were sharing a thought. It wasn't anything special or complicated—it was something a man could think and a dog could think. It was something like . . . "Ahhh!"

Chapter **15**

As *Juno* hit maturity, we thought she seemed a little subdued—which is to say that she did not speed around our loft apartment and carom off the walls as often as previously. Instead of giving thanks, we worried that there was not enough stimulation in her life.

"Maybe she's lonely," we said to each other.

Juno was anything but lonely. She had Sadie the cat. She had Jill. She had me. She had a number of dog friends with whom she romped at the park. She had two or three dog friends who would visit us with their humans, and she would visit them. Add to this her human friends, of which she had more than we did.

"I think she's lonely," we said to each other. "We should get another dog to keep her company."

It's a testament to our sharpness of mind and good judgment that we wound up at Gussik Kennels once again.

Arnold, our second Malamute, was Franz Gussik's

masterpiece. Only selling a dog already dead or made of acrylic would have been more of a coup.

"This pup is special," Franz said.

"He looks sort of scuzzy," I said.

"He's six months old. It's an awkward age for Malamutes. That's why I'm prepared to let him go for a pittance."

"He's sort of runty and scrawny, isn't he?"

"Not at all. In fact, he's big for his size. Here, feel him."

He thrust the puppy into my arms. It licked my face. Jill reached over to hug the puppy and got kissed too. We were goners. We took Arnold with us.

When we got him home and looked at him in a good light, we could see that his head was too big for his body, his tail appeared to be screwed on wrong, and he had a tendency to bump into things. There was nothing right with Arnold. Half his weight was intestinal worms. He had a bad cough. His feet stank, and he would have a fit if he heard a sudden noise.

In time, Arnold calmed down a bit. He didn't hit the ceiling whenever a truck rolled by. He grew into proportion and got to be downright handsome. He also began to exhibit a sort of charm and . . . well . . . suavity and elegance.

But he also began to show a side we never dreamed he had: He turned into a fighter. He didn't fight with Juno. She had wisely begun to intimidate him from the first day, and he never lost his respect for her quick tooth. Arnold's potential opponents—actually his victims—were all dogs on earth other than Juno.

Our best guess is that during Arnold's first six months, he'd been abused in various ways by humans and dogs. Now he was evening the score. Malamutes were bred to pull freight. It's not unheard of for them to move a ton in weight-pulling contests. If Arnold saw a German shepherd he wanted to destroy while being walked on a leash, it took some doing to keep it from happening.

We must have read a hundred books about dog training. I consulted numerous experts. Some of these people were remarkable. They had brilliant theories about how Arnold got to be so antisocial. None of them had any useful suggestions about how to turn him around.

One trainer suggested a method. First we'd have to find another aggressive Malamute whose owner wanted a cure. Then we'd muzzle the two of them so they couldn't harm each other, tie them together by the collar with a cord two feet long, and throw them into a closet for an hour or so. This way they'd get it out of their system, the trainer explained. They'd try to fight, get frustrated, fall asleep, wake up, try again, and so forth, until they were sick of the whole business.

We tried it. All that happened was that Arnold learned how to menace another dog while taking a nap. When I peeked into the closet, Arnold was fast asleep, growling loudly, and the other Malamute was crying for its mother.

Next we simply enrolled Arnold in an ordinary dog-obedience class, the kind they have at the local VFW or adult-ed program. We warned the instructor, of course, and Arnold wore his muzzle to class.

These classes are usually held in some gymnasium or similar space, and they're a little like a square dance. The instructor stands in the middle of the room, calling out commands, and the trainees and dogs march around doing his bidding.

At first I simply dragged Arnold around the floor. He'd travel on his back or side much of the time, pawing the air and screaming threats at the other dogs. Occasionally, he'd grovel and paw his way toward some terrified poodle—and I'd drag him away.

Each course lasted six or eight weeks. Arnold went through six courses—all identical, all beginner's obedience. By the third course, I was able to dispense with the muzzle. Arnold continued vocalizing, but I had become so strong and expert in handling the leash that I could control his occasional lunges at some innocent beagle.

Juno, mostly from just watching week after week, had become a sort of obedience genius, and we'd take her out and win trophies with her on weekends.

A full two years after I'd started trying to train Arnold, I took him to an obedience match sponsored by the local Malamute club. It was an all-northern dog match—Siberian huskies, Malamutes, Samoyeds, and Akitas—all of them feisty and scrappy by nature. The match was held indoors; space was limited, and Arnold brushed up against a number of tough customers.

He never raised a lip to any of them, even though he had several explicit invitations. When it was his turn to compete, he turned in a record low score. People must have thought I was crazy, beaming with pride as I was.

On the way home, I bought Arnold his very own Big Mac and a milk shake—as I had promised him I'd do if he kept his choppers off the other dogs at the match.

It was possible to live with Arnold after that. He was never perfect, but he had some remarkable qualities. I wouldn't want to go through the experience of training a crazy animal again, but I'm glad I did it once. He taught me a lot, that dog.

Chapter 16

Once, Jill had fun with Arnold by pretending that she was teaching him a nursery song. It was pure nonsense—Jill was tending our old-fashioned nonautomatic clothes washer, and Arnold was keeping her company. Jill sang him the song about the eensy-beensy spider and indicated where he was supposed to join in. He did so with something between a scream of anguish and the call of a moose in rut.

The next time Jill had laundry to do, Arnold appeared and sat squirming excitedly until she sang him the song. He came in on cue. Arnold learned a number of songs. His vocal range was limited, but his ear was good.

It was also Arnold who taught Juno to set up a howl whenever we passed a McDonald's. On one vacation trip, we had breakfasted on Egg McMuffins for a week, and the dogs always got an English muffin. They never forgot.

I once observed Arnold taking care of an eight-week-old kitten. The kitten was in a cage. Arnold wanted to go and sleep in his private corner, but every time the kitten cried, Arnold would drag himself to his feet, slouch over to the cage, and lie down with his nose between the wires so the kitten could sink in its tiny claws. When the kitten became quiet, Arnold would head for his corner and flop, exhausted. Immediately the kitten would cry, and Arnold would haul himself back to the cage. I counted this performance repeated over forty times.

Arnold acquired friends. People would visit him. They would borrow Arnold sometimes and drive to the White Castle and feed him hamburgers.

He was the sort of dog you could talk things over with. But he was not just a good listener, affable eccentric, and bon vivant. He was a magnificent athlete. While Juno was tireless and efficient on the trail, Arnold made locomotion an art—a ballet.

Watching Arnold run flat-out in a large open space was unforgettable, and it opened a window to something exceedingly ancient and precious: a link to the first time men followed dogs and hunted to live. He was a splendid companion—and he would pull you up a steep hill if you were tired.

In a way, the hardest thing about living with dogs in modern times is related to the excellent care we give them. Vast sums are spent by pet-food companies devising beautifully balanced, cheap, palatable diets. Vet care today is superb, and most pet owners take advantage of it. As a result, dogs live longer, surviving illnesses that they would not have survived in earlier times. And it very often falls to us to decide when a dog's life has to end—when suffering has come to outweigh satisfaction.

When it came Arnold's time to die, it was I who decided it. I called the vet and told him I was bringing Arnold in.

The vet knew about Malamute vigor. He prepared a syringe with twice the dose it would take to put a dog Arnold's size to sleep. "Put to sleep" is an apt euphemism. It's simply an overdose of a sleeping drug. The dog feels nothing.

"There's enough in here for a gorilla," the vet wisecracked weakly. He was uncomfortable with what he had to do. Arnold, of course, was completely comfortable, doing his best to put everyone else at ease.

I held Arnold while the vet tied off a vein. "This will take six, maybe eight, seconds at most," the vet said. He injected the fluid.

Nothing happened. Arnold, who had been completely relaxed, was now somewhat intent—not unconscious, not dead.

"Sometimes it takes a little longer," the vet said. It had been a full half-minute. Arnold was looking around.

The vet was perspiring. I knew what he was thinking. Some ghastly error. The wrong stuff in the syringe. More than a minute had passed.

A crazy thought occurred to me. Was it possible?

Was Arnold waiting for me to give him leave to go? I rubbed his shoulders and spoke to him. "It's okay, Arnold. I release you." Instantly he died.

I swear I felt his spirit leave his body.

The vet and I went outside and cried for a quarter of an hour.

He was an awfully good dog.

Chapter 17

In pre-Jill days, I used to attend parties at the classy West Village apartment of a couple who were the only collectors of my art. I got free eats and drinks and someplace warm to spend an evening. They got a real live artist with a big mustache, and a single man, to fix up with one of their many unmarried female friends.

On one occasion, I got talking to the wrong girl. My host took me aside.

"She's not the one you were supposed to meet."

"So? She's nice."

"She's an editor. You don't want to talk to her."

"I don't?"

"No! Do you want to ruin your reputation?"

"Editors are bad?"

"Of course they're bad."

"But you're an editor yourself."

"And do you think I'm proud of that?"

He needn't have worried. We were only talking business. The editor, a children's book editor, was looking for some art to go with a book of African stories, and I had just come back from helping to set up an artist's workshop and cooperative in Tanzania. I had what she needed.

When she came to look at the African stuff, she also saw my work.

"You could illustrate a picture book," she said.

"I could? Does it pay anything?"

"Well, you'd split with the writer—an advance against royalties of fifteen hundred dollars."

Why split with anyone? I thought. I'll write the thing myself and pick up some easy money.

In that moment, I became a writer. It would take years, however, for me to respond to popular outrage and quit doing the illustrations. But I was able to get more children's books published, even with my drawings. My experiences at Glade and Glen, and teaching art to kids in various settlement-house basements and attics around Manhattan, all figured in. I had a point of view. I had a knack. And I had a profession. By the time Jill turned up and our menagerie got under way, I was earning enough to justify staying home at the typewriter while Jill hired out as a professor at, among other places, the police academy in New York. She never answered my questions as to whether grading takes on a different aspect when your students are all armed.

For much of this period, Arnold's education went

forward. He was forever a remedial student due to his tendency to aggress. Since Juno got to be so good at the moves from just hanging around through all the classes, the obedience instructor took to using her as a demonstration dog. After a while, he began using us as demonstration people. Finally, we became his unpaid

assistants, taking slow people and unruly dogs aside and working with them until they caught on. By now, Arnold could participate, in a limited way, in intermediate obedience. (The idea of letting him work off the leash in the presence of other dogs remained too horrible—even though he was calm much of the time and obeyed the commands, the sociopath was lurking just below the surface, and we all knew it.)

For a number of years, Jill and I enjoyed a weekly drive to colorful Union City, New Jersey. A local radio station broadcast programs-of-the-past on Wednesday nights, so we'd listen to *The Shadow* or *The Green Hornet* on the way. With the dogs ensconced in our car, for which I'd designed and built sturdy window grilles so they'd have ventilation in warm weather, we'd visit our favorite Cuban-Chinese restaurant, and after egg fu yung con frijoles, we'd head for the VFW hall where the obedience classes were held.

As much to accommodate the questions of our students as for any other reason, we had joined the local and national Malamute clubs and attended events and competitions on weekends. We worked constantly with our own dogs. Juno became a very competent performer, and for Arnold, reviews were the order of every day. We kept up with advancements in the field and attended workshops and seminars for professional trainers and handlers.

One day, Louie the obedience instructor fired us.

"This is my hobby," he said. "I'm supposed to be

having fun here. I know a lot more about dogs than youse two, but youse guys talk better. You're better with the humans than me. People are starting to come in asking for youse. You're getting a reputation. Frankly, I miss being the center of attention. So don't come back here anymore."

Fair enough. It was his dog-obedience class to begin with, and he'd taught us a lot. But what about our Wednesday routine? We were left with a big hole in the middle of the week.

Chapter **18**

In 1905 the *Hoboken Evening News,* now defunct, put up a magnificent building at 22 Hudson Place. It was the last word in masonry and timber industrial architecture. Five tall stories high, it was eighty-eight feet long and twenty-five feet wide. There was ornamental carved brick on the Hudson Place end, and the rear of the building, which communicated with the cobbled alley separating it from the boat-shaped Hoboken Land and Improvement Company building, had rose windows flanking a large Romanesque arch on the third floor—probably the office of the editor in chief or a boardroom. On the roof there were two immense skylights, guaranteed by their manufacturer not to leak for one thousand years.

When Jill and I bought the building, these had long since been tarred and roofed over, and they leaked anyway. Hoboken had a federally funded urban renewal program in the late sixties, and we were encouraged by a grant of a thousand dollars.

We were already living in the building, which had seen hard use over the decades. The newspaper occupied it for only five years or so before being acquired by another paper. The building was said to have been, at various times, a hotel, a dormitory for soldiers preparing to embark for Europe during World War I (troops left and returned through the port—the origin of the expression "Hell or Hoboken by Christmas"), a civilian flophouse, a light-manufacturing site with sweatshops on each floor, and, when we bought it and resided there, living lofts.

Living lofts are a feature of life in New York City and adjacent places like Brooklyn and Hoboken. They must exist in other cities, but not possibly in such numbers, or with such complex laws and culture grown up around them. Put simply, they are industrial spaces converted into dwellings. Artists prize them because of their high ceilings and space, and there is a subcategory of "artists' lofts," which are legal as studios but not as residences. The visitor to lower Manhattan will see buildings with signs at various levels reading A.I.R. (Artist in Residence), denoting a legal living loft and alerting the New York Fire Department not to let the building burn to the ground without attempting rescue.

Many nineteenth-century industrial and commercial buildings survive in old parts of town, particularly on the waterfront. Five stories or less, and without elevators, they're ideal for artists or people who simply like living in enormous rooms.

There were virtually no traces of elegance on the inside of 22 Hudson Place when we bought it. The arched window was there, but if there had been high-class flooring, or paneled offices, or any gracious touches, they were gone. There was a gang shower on the second floor, a leftover from the building's military and flop-house periods, no doubt. In the basement, two oil-fired boilers, one huge and the other gargantuan, supplied hot water and heat. Either of them could have powered the *Queen Mary*. The basement also contained four or five disheveled and confused men who had been living there for God knows how long. Explaining to them that concerns of fire safety and insurance compelled me to evict them from my basement was the first of many unique experiences I had as an urban property owner.

Some of these experiences were conversations with John, the proprietor of the aptly named the Mercury Restaurant on the first floor. Mercury was what it was actually called, but other names for it could have included Roach and Bun, the Grease Trap, or McPtomaine's. John was fond of saying, "You have to eat a peck of dirt before you die." This he said to outraged customers who had suddenly sobered up, realized what sort of place they were in, and endeavored to complain.

While the front or public parts of the Mercury Restaurant would cause a person who wasn't drunk, or had the power of sight intact, to be staggered by a sudden rush of disgust and a sense of unreality, the hidden part, the kitchen (I shudder to write the word), was frightening to a horrible degree. I had nightmares about it. Grease coated the walls and dripped from the ceiling. The shapes of familiar objects—tables, iceboxes, a stove—were obscured and made hideous by grease. Grease from the Roosevelt administration. Primordial grease. Grease perhaps already generating life-forms never known before.

At first I tried to get John to clean up. He completely failed to comprehend. He wanted to know why I never ate in his restaurant. Then I offered to hire men to clean up. He countered by telling me that no men with that kind of courage and resolve existed. Left no choice, I called the Department of Public Health and summoned the inspector.

"Boss, the inspector came, like you told me he would," John said. "I paid him plenty, okay, boss?" John was missing the point. I tried bribing the inspector myself, the idea being that he would then do a straight inspection. But this was too much of a departure from everything he had ever known. He wrote John some violations, John bribed him, and life went on as it had since the ancestors of these men had crawled out of the Hudson River and begun to lose their gills, two or three generations earlier.

Next I simply offered John money to go away. A thousand didn't do it. Two thousand didn't do it. At three thousand, I was reaching my limit, and John was expressing sadness. "Boss, are you saying you don't like me?" he asked.

Chapter 19

John got busted! It turned out he had been running an illegal poker game in the kitchen, and the state cops surveilled him. They got the goods on him.

My own first thought was "Dear God! They were sitting in the kitchen?"

But John fled. He committed flight to evade prosecution. The Mercury was abandoned, his rent wasn't paid, and he was gone.

Now all I had to do was clean it out.

A small, wiry man named Attila was my salvation. After four or five industrial mess-cleaning firms turned me down flat, Attila appeared. "I swim through filth," he said.

Attila and his sons ripped out everything, counters, cabinets, appliances. After a week, the former Mercury Restaurant was empty and decontaminated, and I will be forever sorry I watched.

The Mercury stood empty for a few months. Times

were bad in Hoboken—its local recession was entering its third decade—and there wasn't a tenant to be had. Besides, the restaurant needed time to settle after the violence that was done, for it was said that where Attila and his sons had demolished, the grass would never grow again. The powerful solvents and military-grade roach killers needed to dissipate, and I needed to forget.

It was in this stretch of time, known as the Post-Mercury Period, that Jill and I were fired from our unpaid gig as assistant dog-obedience instructors.

We missed the Wednesday-night class in Union City. We missed our pupils, drawn from all parts of northern New Jersey, misbred, shambling, flea-ridden, drooling, and bad-smelling though they were. And we missed their dogs too.

We thought we might set up as dog trainers in a small way. We could handle it if we didn't try to take on anything really difficult. And we could set up the Mercury as a canine classroom.

You don't need a lot of equipment to train dogs. We slapped paint on the walls, put down some rubber runners for the dogs to trot around on, dragged in some odds and ends of furniture, tacked up some doggy posters, and we were ready! I painted an almost professional-looking sign that read SUPERPUPPY. We ran the cheapest possible classified ad in *The Jersey Journal*: "We train you to train your dog. Superpuppy. $35. 555-1234." We were in business.

Now began the real learning. We had handled more

than a hundred dogs in Union City, maybe as many as two hundred. They were all individuals belonging to individual humans and families who had specific expectations and limitations. Every one taught us something. But since we weren't the ones in charge—we had Louie the instructor's superior experience to fall back on—we didn't absolutely have to get results.

It was different when it was our own show. Somehow the fact of being the last word and locally supreme authority caused us to look harder, think more, seek clues to the personality and background of each dog—and person. I noticed the same thing when I suddenly and precipitously launched myself into writing. I'd written plenty through sixteen years of school, but it was a different story when strangers were going to pay me, and other strangers were going to read the stuff.

To underscore this, our first clients were just about the best we possibly could have had. A well-dressed man with a notably nice Great Dane pup and a son about eleven came in. "This is my puppy, and this is my son," he said. "Train them."

Everything about this guy suggested he knew what he was doing. I asked him a lot of questions. It turned out this dog was the family's third Great Dane. The first had lived to the age of eighteen. The second was poisoned at fifteen and died at sixteen. It's well known that Danes peg out at about age nine. How is it that his were getting a double dip? I asked him.

"It's easy," he said. "Any dog starts lying around,

snoozing and goofing, at about eighteen months. We just don't let our dogs do that. We get out on the bike every day, and the dog comes with us. Our dogs aren't allowed to get flabby hearts like old athletes."

The dog's name was Barkley. I forget the name of the kid. They came once a week for their six-lesson course and left us a precision-tuned, synchronized pair. That they were *en rapport* and having a good time with each other stuck out a mile. They never needed us. The kid's father knew more than we did—he just subscribed to the idea that certain things like driving, golf, and dog training should be learned from someone unrelated.

Chapter 20

Had we given it any thought, we might have suspected that Barkley and his young master were angels in disguise, or hirelings of the Hoboken Chamber of Commerce making sure that we gave our small business a fair shake and did not become discouraged at how very weird it all was. Of course we suspected no such thing of the pair and saw them off, dog and lad, with their Superpuppy diploma and our best wishes.

We never dealt with anyone else remotely sane for the next two years. I have to say, the citizens of Hudson County, New Jersey, were, for the most part, lovable—if well beyond the reach of logic. There was Blueboy, a Great Dane. The father of the family had dreamed all his life of owning such a dog, and now that he was in failing health, his family had bought him one. Father, mother, sons, daughters, an old grandmother from Europe, and a couple of aunts came along for every session with us. Blueboy had better bloodlines than the family and was treated like a nobleman who was visiting a peasant home. He had no need of training, since he was allowed to do whatever he wanted. This could have been a problem if he hadn't been completely sweet-natured, wanting nothing but to lean against people lovingly. That and to eat. What did he eat? (We used to ask questions like that and work in a little nutrition information and basic health care along with the obedience lessons.) For breakfast Blueboy ate toast, medium, with a little butter, coffee—extremely light—and eggs the way he liked them. And how did Blueboy like his eggs? Scrambled, loose, with a little salt, no pepper. How did they determine that this, out of all the ways to prepare eggs, was the Dane's favorite? The old grandmother beamed toothlessly . . . trial and error.

The family did not care if Blueboy ever learned to heel, and they never practiced with him. He came to school because . . . what? He should be denied an education? If they could have gotten him into Princeton, he would have gone—they all would have gone.

Each week, Blueboy and his loving family came to our school, and Blueboy would lean against me, and we would talk about what a fine dog he was.

A desperate-looking Vietnam-era burnout turned up with a carton of Chihuahua puppies. "These dogs have to be trained," he said. "If they don't learn control, they can grow up to be killers."

So I sat cross-legged on the floor, lined the mouselike puppies up before me, and, waving my forefingers as if

I were conducting a miniature orchestra, I taught them to sit on command.

"I appreciate what you're doing," their owner said. "You'll do me a favor if you don't go easy on them. They need to learn restraint. I don't want them turning vicious."

Not every customer was as entertaining. There were the idiots with the profoundly deaf dog. I taught the dog to work to hand signals, and she nearly exploded with joy when she realized communication was possible. The family gave up on the dog as impossible to housebreak. "She just wouldn't *listen*," they said.

There was Ralph Kramden, the Jersey City bus driver with an impish husky. She was goofing all over him.

"So what do I do?" he asked me. "The dog is making a monkey of me."

"You look her in the eye," I said. "You take the first and second fingers of your right hand, and you give her a little snap, right across the schnozzola. Just do it once. She'll get the idea."

The next week, here came Ralphie. "I sure surprised her," he said. "I picked her up bodily and threw her across the living room. She bounced off the fireplace."

"You did *what*?" I was beside myself. "You could have crippled her! You could have killed her!"

"Well, you said I could hit her."

That was the last time I ever did that. You have to be extremely careful what you say. You never know when people are listening. Oh, and by the way, YOU ARE NOT ALLOWED TO HIT YOUR DOG.

Just making sure.

There was the Hoboken Goldilocks who came in wearing work gloves and dragging an enormous shepherdoid by a hunk of chain.

"The dog, he chews on my hands," she said.

The dog obliged by doing so, drooling, smiling.

"When he isn't doing that, he chews on my ass!"

He proceeded to demonstrate.

"I have tooth marks all over my ass! I can't go to the beach."

"Miss?"

"What?"

"Tell him to stop doing that."

"So do you think you can help me? I mean, he doesn't mean any harm, but he's so strong. My ass is all black and blue."

"Miss?"

"What?"

"Tell him to stop doing that!"

"My boyfriend thinks it's funny. But I don't think it's funny. I got bruises all over me. We're supposed to go to the shore, and I have this cute bikini, only I can't wear it. It looks like I was in an accident."

"Miss!"

"What?"

"Tell him to stop doing that!"

"So, do you think you can help me?"

"I have my doubts."

Chapter 21

There was a two-stage admission process before one got to be a Superpuppy student. First the phone call, half of which went like this:

"Can you make my dog mean?"

"We don't do that, and we advise against it. Would you keep a loaded and cocked pistol around the house?"

"What's your point?"

So that took care of 50 percent of prospective pupils. Then there was the interview. I found that a change had taken place in me. I was more like all the other dog trainers I had met. I would hear myself saying things like "Madam, you are too stupid to keep a dog. There is nothing we can do for you. Go away."

I had never been rude to people before—never cruel. But that was before I saw the things I saw in my days at Superpuppy.

Here's a little family drama that we encountered

over and over: In comes a mother with two young teenagers, or kids nearly in their teens. And look! Mom is pregnant. A late surprise, just when she thought she was going to get a little break. What has she done? She has brought home a puppy. At a time like this. Around week three of the course, Mom turns up crying. She kicked the pup down some stairs, or whipped the hell out of it with a belt.

We would tell her to simply walk away. Leave the puppy with us—we would find it a good home. We'd try to assure her she had done no permanent harm, and that this just wasn't a good time to have a puppy around.

Another scenario: Dad has always felt deep down that his ancestors in Europe were of royal blood. Now that he has the suburban house, the upscale cars, the blazer with the crest, he gets himself a Russian wolf-hound, or a Marrema sheepdog, or a Kuvasz, or a mastiff—something purebred and classy, and difficult, requiring more experience than he's got, and more patience. And this dog is going to be perfect. He's going to enter it in dog shows and obedience matches, and if it doesn't perform, he's going to take it behind some bushes and whip the hell out of it. On an occasion or two, I caught the Lord of One-and-a-Half Landscaped Acres in the act and suggested to him that I might do to him like he was doing to little Prince Valiant of Parsippany. I weighed three hundred pounds in those days and was very active.

There was the brilliant nine-year-old with the brilliant miniature schnauzer. She exhausted our store of things to teach—and by the end, we were inventing circus routines for her. However, at nine the little girl wasn't awake late enough or in a position to take on the housebreaking—Mom had to do that but wasn't able to make the effort. So at the end of the course, they gave the dog away.

When a mother and daughter and German short-haired pointer came to see us all the way from Brooklyn, I first suggested that I direct them to an ethical and capable instructor closer to home. They weren't interested. They wanted to train with us. I agreed, but only on the condition that they pay half our usual fee.

After they had signed up and left, and a bit confused, Jill asked me why I had done that.

"Well, she's a nice woman, and the child is very bright and pleasant. The dog is excellent and only wants to be schooled, it isn't sick in body or mind. They're going to be a pleasure to work with, and I know you especially enjoy dealing with the kids. I just couldn't charge them full price."

"You realize," Jill said, "you just gave them a fifty percent discount for being normal."

They were the last students we signed up. We closed the school and wrote up what we'd learned in a book, *Superpuppy,* still in print after something like twenty-five years. We turned from the honest and useful trade of teaching people how to better enjoy dogs, to the less admirable one of writing. Still, someone has to do it.

Chapter 22

Jill and I were sitting in the living room of a librarian in Flagstaff, Arizona. The librarian was entertaining us after I had given a speech to the local librarians' association. We were making small talk. It was pro forma. In a few more minutes Jill and I would leave in our rental car and go back to our motel.

I was sitting by an open window. Suddenly, through the screen, I saw a pair of penetrating almond-shaped yellow eyes gazing at me.

"What the hell is that?" I said—or some other witty remark.

"Oh, that big dog comes around every night," the librarian said. "Pretty, isn't he?"

Pretty he was, and big—and a dog perhaps in part. What I saw was predominantly wolf. Probably one of those wolf-dog crosses that unenlightened people breed. The results are almost always tragic: dogs with some of the more problematic traits of wolves—wariness, nervousness, a sort of delicacy; or wolves with some of the less appealing characteristics of dogs—rowdiness, aggression, destructiveness. This individual appeared to be all wolf. Only his fearless approach suggested anything else.

"Jill," I said quietly. "Change seats with me and talk to this animal."

I had long known Jill to be one of those people who can communicate with animals. She can get close enough to deer to almost touch them. Birds circle around her. There are always a couple of crows that follow her around and sit in branches just above her head. She has friends among squirrels, Canada geese, and skunks. None of this is by accident. She comes on to critters, wild and domestic. She coos to them, and they fall in love. Something of the kind happened to me once upon a time.

I knew that Jill had always wanted to have a one-on-one conversation with a wolf. While I distracted the librarian, Jill put her face close to the screen and chatted the creature up. I saw the familiar besotted expression appear in its eyes. Its tail was waving side to side delightedly.

After a while the wolf couldn't stand it anymore and bounded off into the night.

When we were taking our leave, I held the librarian back at the door, making last-minute remarks, giving Jill a chance to move into the darkness and across the road.

She was barely visible to me, just a dark silhouette. I

saw another dark shape appear from nowhere and fly at her—something big. Jill and the wolf sank to the ground, hugging, wrestling. The librarian was nattering about something under the porch light. I watched over her shoulder as Jill and the wolf bonded. The wolf had behaved precisely as the animal-behavior books indicated it should. It had turned its head sideways, offered its throat, kissed Jill's face. In a few minutes, the wolf, having had its say, disappeared into the hills—probably to kill an elk and drag it back as an offering for his new love object.

The next day we were in the neighborhood, asking local kids about the wolf. It turned out to belong to a centerfold type who kept it in a little yard behind her apartment. The wolf would regularly get loose and range in the nearby hills. The cops and the volunteer fire-department guys were only too happy to bring the wolf back to the girl, who would reward them with cold beer and a look at her crocheted bikini.

Jill hatched a plan to wolfnap the thing but thought better of it. We returned that night, and the wolf turned up for an enthusiastic reunion with Jill. I was introduced, and acknowledged, because of who I was with—still an honor for me. But that was as far as it went. We did not go back east with a semidomesticated *Canis lupus* at that time.

Chapter 23

It had been about a year and a half since Arnold had died. We were living in a little house on Long Island with Juno and a bunch of cats. Jill had acquired two Icelandic horses, a mother and a foal. This is such a whole other story that I am not going to say another word about it, except that the horses came to be quartered in a pasture with a little shed, a remnant of the last dairy farm in town. This was a couple of miles from the house, and Jill or I would go to tend the horses at least twice a day.

Jill came back from a horse-care errand one day and told me she had seen a dog running free who bore an amazing resemblance to Arnold. She had asked a local if he knew the dog and was assured that it was around the neighborhood all the time. She muttered something under her breath about people who let their dogs run loose, and went about her business.

The next morning when Jill arrived at the dairy,

there was the Malamute, lying dead in the driveway. A knot of people stared at the pathetic spectacle, while a little mongrel stood guard over the body. People were clucking their tongues and observing what a beautiful dog, though dead. When the little mongrel's owner came by and collected his dog, Jill was able to get closer to the body. She noticed a paw twitch slightly, and her suspicions were confirmed: This was not a dead Malamute. This was a sleeping Malamute, which is practically the same thing. Jill gave a whistle, and the dog stopped being dead and hopped into her car. This was Arctic Flake, who would trail after Jill like a shadow for the next decade. Juno's response, and that of the cats, was instant and casual acceptance. It was as though Arnold had come back. They greeted the new dog and settled in as if she had never not been with us. The local who had recognized her now allowed that he had never seen her before. No one was looking for a dog of her description at the pound, and we sighed with relief when a week passed and no one responded to the ad we ran in the paper.

Unlike Arnold, Flake had no aggression problem. In fact, there was never an occasion when she might have felt the need to show aggression. Other dogs seemed to defer to her automatically. She was relaxed, perpetually bemused, and always in charge.

Jill's wild and woolly college roommate, Caitlin, visited us from the West. "Well, no wonder. What you have there is a wolf hybrid." I refused to buy this and deny it to this day. The fact that Caitlin had raised a number of wolf-dogs was barely excused by her being beautiful and exotic. I am against wolf hybrids, and Flake was not one. Caitlin had lived in a tepee and had partaken of many herbs and natural substances, and I am not obliged to accept her opinions.

Flake's effect on domestic dogs suggested they would have agreed with Caitlin, but that also proves nothing. And if Flake was a wolf cross, she was one of the terribly rare stable ones, and certainly not evidence that such an experiment is a good idea.

What Arctic Flake was, for sure, was a devoted presence shuffling along at Jill's side for so many years, quiet, observant, and kind. She was patient with various dogs who came our way. I remember her indulgence of Bear, a black chow chow who spent the months of his puppyhood hanging by his teeth from Flake's ruff, like a Mexican trapeze artist. He had to be as foreign to her as any canine could be—he certainly was to me. As a chow chow, he had almost no facial expression, moved differently from most dogs, smelled entirely different, had a blue tongue, had fat undoglike feet, would lie silent and unmoving for long periods of time, and was . . . well, inscrutable. Yet Flake raised him, odd as he was.

Flake's passion was food, and her mode of exercising that passion was theft. All sled dogs are thieves, and Flakey was a master. The only time she would leave Jill's side was when she slipped off the property to raid a few garbage cans. She knew how to open the refrigerator but didn't do it often enough for us to feel constrained to figure out a way to secure it. Most ways to secure things didn't present much of a problem for Flake anyway.

When Flake died, Jill missed her badly. As Flake had turned up and seemingly replaced Arnold, Jill hoped for Flake's replacement to turn up, and she scanned the horizon for such an animal for five years.

Chapter **24**

Before Flake died, we moved to a farm in the Hudson Valley. The only livestock to come with the place was a truly enormous old hen, who, typically enough, fixated on Jill and followed her everywhere, making what I assumed to be affectionate chicken noises. This was not to last long, as Juno and Arctic Flake executed a neat pincer movement and dispatched old Henrietta in what I believe they regarded as their finest adventure together.

Juno lived to be about half again as old as Malamutes are supposed to get. Her last couple of years were spent in a sort of happy haze, watching leaves fall, or snowflakes, each one a complete novelty. Everything amused her. She may not have been compos mentis, but her digestion was fine, and her heart was strong, and she appeared completely happy.

When Juno finally checked out, I was without a special dog of my own. Arctic Flake graciously tried to divide her time between Jill and me—she'd turn up in my office, where she never used to hang out, and try to be sociable. I played along and even took her on a few walks, but it was evident she was thinking about Jill the whole time.

Bear, the black chow chow, may have regarded himself as my dog. However, he was a spectacularly self-contained little chap, and his emotions were expressed by visiting me in my office once or twice a week and bestowing upon me exactly one wag of the tail and one dab of the tongue. His primary activity appeared to be meditation. He was a student of Zen, or some other esoteric practice based on nonattachment. Bear could spend hour upon hour lying chow chow–fashion, stubby front legs extended before him, stubby hind legs extended behind, counting his breaths, and regarding the illusory nature of experience. He had bad hips and couldn't go on long walks. I took him for car rides. It was a low-intensity relationship.

Every so often, I would take a walk through the local animal shelter. I told myself it was a holdover from my dog-training days. I'd size up the available talent. Sometimes I'd spot a dog with extra potential, and Jill and I would sponsor it—underwrite some of the expenses, offer some free training to whoever would adopt it, donate a copy of our dog-care book to make a more appealing package.

Jill didn't join me on these pound visits. She said it was like being a tourist in a concentration camp. I, of course, was there on personal business, though I denied it. I was looking for a dog and didn't even know it.

On one of these visits I came across a three-year-old mongrel. He was a classic pound shepherd, scrawny, medium in size, possibly part collie or Labrador—shelters are full of these. But there was something in this dog's expression—his eyes. I went home and got Jill. I wanted to know if she saw what I saw.

She did.

"You going to take him home?" she asked me.

"No," I said. "That will make three dogs. We've got the horses and a big bunch of cats. We're full up. I thought we'd just offer the book and the free lessons."

"You can take him if you want him," Jill said.

"No, I just wanted you to see him. He'll get a home."

"What if he doesn't?"

"He will."

I don't have to tell you that the shepherd cross came home with Jill when his week was up and he hadn't been adopted.

It was Bastille Day, July 14, when the coughing, twitching, insecure dog, smelling of harsh disinfectant and fear, was brought home. We named him Jacques (full name, Jacques Amo Pooch Cini) in honor of the Glorious Revolution and installed him in the barn, where he made a lot of noise and annoyed the horses.

The vet had judged Jacques to be about three years old and in decent health. He weighed about fifty-eight pounds, had been neutered at some point, was highly nervous, and took an undue interest in scraggly-looking young men, usually shirtless, on loud motor-cycles.

I discovered by accident, when I pulled on a pair of work gloves, that someone had made a pathetic attempt at making a guard dog of Jacques. When he saw the gloves go on, he made a miserable and halfhearted attack on them. His whole body expressed relief when I took off the gloves—his signal that he could stop attacking.

He was not kidding, however, when it came to food. If interrupted or crowded while eating, he would snap in earnest. This fit in with something I noticed about him only when the vet pointed it out to me: Jacques was part Akita. Once it was mentioned, I noticed that wrinkle of the forehead, and the tendency to touch the tips of the ears together, and the goofy pigeon-toed gait, all of which amount to expressions of superiority among Akitas. I admit to a prejudice about dogs of Asian descent—they tend to be ready to bite. I wouldn't have passed Jacques up had I known about his ancestry and his toothiness, but it was clear that he and I had our work cut out for us.

Boot camp for Jacques started on July 15. We spent the whole day together, and a good part of the night. My favorite dog-walking, and training, spot is the Vanderbilt Mansion National Historic Site, situated on high bluffs overlooking the Hudson River. Here we practiced close-order drill, heel, sit, and stay: the ABCs of training. It's not just a matter of getting the dog to obey certain commands—these few basic exercises establish that concepts can be expressed and understood, and that an interspecies language can be developed.

In addition to learning that "Sit!" means sit, Jacques learned that he was admirable and accomplished for knowing it and doing it—also that he *had* to do it every time—because he was Jacques, and entitled to think "I am Jacques. I am he who knows to sit. I am good. I am smart. This is my human, whom I must obey, and who feeds me. When he tells me to sit, I sit, and he admires me for this."

Inculcating that—"I am"—is why I am a good trainer and whoever taught Jacques to attack gloves is an idiot.

If a dog were a scintilla smarter, this whole business would collapse like a house of cards. As a trainer, I count on the dog's inability to place his tongue between his lips and make a noise.

Chapter **25**

Jacques took to the training. He was interested and quick to learn. Also, he was good company. It was clear to me that he enjoyed being with me on the grounds of the old Vanderbilt estate, with the many exotic trees collected by the Vanderbilts' predecessor. Jacques had a dazzling smile—one felt flattered to have it turned one's way. After the training session, we'd reward ourselves with a little walk.

Jacques knew pretty much everything he needed to know after the first week. After the second, he was crisp and precise—when I stepped, he stepped; when I stopped, he sat; when I turned left or right, he wheeled with me, his shoulder an inch from my knee. Moving with a well-trained dog is like dancing with Ginger Rogers.

By the third week, I no longer needed to handle the leash. I draped it over my neck, leaving the end clipped to Jacques's collar in observance of the law. We were training less and walking more. Jacques left the barn and moved into the house. He was getting along with the other animals.

Something I believe in is talking to the dog—a lot—in the course of training. This usually amounts to a lot of "Goooood boy! That's a goooood boy! Are you a goooood boy?" But somehow, in Jacques's case, with that attentive expression and smile, I found myself going into more detail. Jacques and I discussed the foul architecture of the Vanderbilt mansion and commented on the excellent landscaping. We enjoyed the monumental beech trees and observed hawks, and sometimes an eagle, soaring over the Hudson. I helped Jacques overcome his inappropriate enthusiasm for the Vanderbilt squirrels by pretending they were extremely dangerous carnivores. Jacques fell for this, simple creature that he was, and the first of us to see one would crowd against the other, and we would tiptoe past the vicious arboreal rodent whispering cautions.

I believe the other walkers at the Vanderbilt Mansion National Historic Site may have been made a bit uneasy by our animated conversations, especially the whispering and tiptoeing and manifestations of fear of squirrels, but we were too caught up in chatter to pay much attention to them.

Our routine expanded. We'd share a bagel, and I'd have a coffee in the car, and then we'd do four brisk miles. By the end of the summer, Jacques had gone from fifty-eight pounds to ninety, of which every ounce was muscle. Any trace of insecurity was gone, and he had developed many wagging acquaintanceships among the regular Vanderbilt walkers, human and canine.

Jacques turned out to have an eye for the ladies. I speak of human ladies. Right under my nose, he'd carry on a flirtation with this one or that one. All the young women who worked at the vet's office had told me that he was their favorite client. Now, I liked Jacques and appreciated his affable personality, but I knew he wasn't outstandingly cute, and while friendly enough, he didn't seem all *that* charming. Until the time I dropped him off for his bath and saw this: Jacques stood up with one forepaw on the counter, and in the crook of his other forepaw, he took the hand of the young woman and conveyed it to his lips. He kissed it delicately while looking up into her eyes. She reacted as if he were Errol Flynn. He was strutting as she led him off to have his bath and pedicure, swarmed over by the young woman and two of her colleagues. He couldn't have been doing any better if he had handed them long-stemmed roses.

Another young woman, who cleaned house for us, held Jacques in special regard. Once, attempting a joke, I said, "You know, he has other girlfriends."

"It's all right," she said, "because . . . I think I've met someone."

Jacques and I did the Vanderbilt walk in all conditions except active blizzards every morning for ten years. He was never bored, and neither was I.

I had been asked to write an article for a local regional magazine. I wrote about taking a morning walk with Jacques at the Vanderbilt Mansion National Historic Site in Hyde Park—your basic utilitarian essay about the flora and fauna we see, and what a good dog Jacques was. The magazine decided to run a couple of pictures, so Jacques and I turned up at the Vanderbilt to meet the photographer.

Obviously Jacques couldn't conceptualize photography. He couldn't know that we were making pictures, but he had no trouble figuring out that he was getting attention and approval by striking poses. The magazine editor had asked for a shot of Jacques walking, showing me only from the knees down.

The photographer got down on the ground and had us walk past her many times. The idea was that she'd snap the picture when Jacques was right in front of her. As we made each pass, I'd hear her chuckle. I asked her what was funny, and she told me that Jacques was turning his head toward her and shooting her a grin at the precise moment, every time.

Next we moved Jacques to a stone pedestal in front of the mansion. He instantly assumed the library lion pose and gave the photographer his best profile, and a smile just short of grotesque. I was in the pictures too, but only as scenery. It was no work. All I had to do was not squint.

After a few parapet shots, Jacques had an idea. He crawled forward and dangled his paws over the edge.

Then he crossed his legs. Then he inclined his head toward me, confidentially, always with the dazzling smile.

We did some car shots. Jacques had been strictly trained not to protrude so much as his nose out the car window. Dogs who ride with their heads hanging out can get eye injuries from airborne debris. The photographer asked me if I could get Jacques to stick his head out the window.

"I'll try," I said. "He's conditioned not to do that."

Even as I spoke, he was half out the window, doing his impression of FDR.

When we got home, Jacques was tired and napped heavily. Modeling, at a certain level, is not posing—it is acting.

When the photographer came by the next day to show us the slides, all the throw-outs were marred by something I had done: blinking, moving, looking stupid. Jacques was perfect in every single exposure.

Jacques was a good friend to me and taught me many things, mostly the things dogs always teach us about loyalty, and consistency of affection, and appreciating a friend. He also demonstrated how to live and enjoy life right up to the day of one's death.

He was quite the gentleman.

Chapter 26

Jill got to be friendly with Jane, the animal control officer—a woman whose uniform had the sharpest creases I've ever seen. She enforced the laws and showed no favor to anyone. She would have arrested her own mother. She judged her fellow citizens strictly by how well they cared for their animals and how responsible they were. Jill was at the top of Jane's very short list of the respectable and the righteous. (Because of some aberration I do not understand, 100 percent of people seem to assume that all virtues Jill and I have as a couple have to do with her and not me. Why is that?)

One day I looked out the window and saw the sun glinting off Jane's collar ornaments. She had pulled up in the spotless animal control truck and was having a little chat with Jill. It seemed that Jane had caught Old Diablo, the most notorious stray dog in the county.

Old Diablo's master had died five years earlier, and

the dog had become feral, making his living by raiding garbage cans. He was expert at evading capture and knew tricks like running the wrong way up a one-way street when being pursued by a vehicle. None of the animal wardens in the surrounding towns had been able to bring in Old Diablo. Jane had caught him.

She would. Of course it was her duty, we can't have stray dogs all over the place, but my sympathies were with Diablo. Since he was so good at making his own living, why not give him a pass?

Jill wanted to have a look at him, so off we went to the pound. I had misgivings. I could see how this might play out. If there were a ghost of a chance of rehabilitating him, Jill was going to bring him home. My heart sank, and my knees ached at the thought of dealing with an animal who was probably smarter than I was.

It turned out there wasn't a chance of rehabilitating Old Diablo. He was wilder than wild, shifting from foot to foot, keeping his head low, growling softly. His eyes glowed dully like two red-hot setting suns.

"I trusted a human once, and he died," the dog was saying. "Now that you've caught me, you have to kill me. I'll never let any of you touch me." I had a momentary thought of sneaking back at night and turning him loose to continue his outlaw life—maybe there was another dog somewhere he would allow to get near him.

As we left the pound we encountered Melvin, an idiot in a feed cap. Melvin was slobbering over an al-

most
grown
yellow
Labrador puppy.

"I've been out here for two hours," Melvin blubbered. "I can't take her in there."

"What's the problem?" Jill asked. She was frustrated because she hadn't been able to do anything for Old Diablo, and Melvin's puppy was cute.

"She makes pee-pee in the house," Melvin said. Melvin was about six feet four, with tattoos.

"Well, that's a problem easily solved," Jill said. "We can give you a few pointers, if you like." By now I had taken the puppy's lead and was walking her around, sizing her up. Nice puppy.

"It's too late," Melvin whimpered. "My wife said don't come home with her. She's fed up."

The puppy's name was Maxine. She came to live with us.

Now an old dog, Maxine is with us to this day. She was a reasonably trainable puppy, though she didn't show any particular talent, was a bit noisy for my taste, and caused a tremendous rivalry between Jacques and Bear. But in general she fitted in. I didn't pay a lot of attention to her once she settled—and to tell the truth, I wasn't terribly attached to her.

People who knew a lot about bird dogs seemed to think she was a good one, but I didn't know enough to see it. She seemed to be just one of the crowd, and of more interest to the other dogs than she was to me.

Later, Maxine would prove just how superior and useful she was, demonstrate marvelous judgment, and earn my gratitude and respect. But for the first few years, I tossed her the occasional biscuit and gave her the occasional pat on the head.

It was the floppy ears. I wasn't used to a dog with floppy ears. They gave her a comical appearance, hence I dismissed her as being of no importance. This was how much insight I had developed after studying dogs for twenty years.

Chapter 27

Jill took me to see some Malamutes at a kennel in Connecticut. We used to do this kind of thing every so often when our spirits needed raising. In this particular period, we had no Malamutes as part of our household. It was Jacques and Maxine by that time. Fine dogs, and good friends to us, but we were missing sled dogs.

Around Malamutes, we always feel a hookup with something extremely ancient and deep—the day when the bond between Man and Dog was still new. When we all lived in packs and hunted to survive. Somehow, being around them makes the very air in our lungs feel fresher, more enlivening.

If a person doesn't feel that special connection, having such a dog is not recommended. They're too much trouble as pets to make it worthwhile. But if you do feel it . . . well, nothing else is quite the same.

There were loads of puppies to play with, and many

splendid adult Malamutes. It was a model kennel. These dogs were from old and exalted lineage. They were in vivid good health and had sparkling personalities. Visiting with them in the tree-lined half-acre backyard and kennel complex was as soul-restoring as we knew it would be.

What Jill knew, and what I had not been told, was that the people who kept these Malamutes also kept a wolf. This was a 100 percent genuine timber wolf, formerly a zoo wolf. The people were credentialed by the state, the Smithsonian, the Humane Society, the Connecticut Board of Rabbis, and I don't know who else to be official wolf-keepers.

"So, you want to see the wolf?" they asked.

"What wolf?"

"We have to put all the dogs into their kennels before we let the wolf out."

"Wolf? Out? What wolf out?"

"The dogs are all put away. We're letting the wolf out!"

"You're letting the wolf out?"

"The wolf is out! The wolf is out!"

"Where? I don't see any wolf."

"I have to tell you," the female of the kennel couple said. "She doesn't like men."

"Doesn't like men? The wolf doesn't like men? I can't see the wolf. Where's the wolf? She doesn't like men?"

The wolf was being invisible. I scoured the small

area, the few trees, the wire-mesh kennels. I saw no wolf.

Then the wolf quit being invisible. She became visible directly in front of me, as though she had materialized on the spot. A real wolf.

Whoever thought up that INTER CANEM ET LUPUM thing—the Hour of the Wolf, connoting the balance point of twilight, which is when you can't distinguish a dog from a wolf—has been totally misunderstood. It had to mean total darkness because, confronted by a real, very tall, well-over-hundred-pound timber wolf, there is no way anyone could mistake it for a dog—at any distance. Even the Malamutes we'd just been enjoying, the most wolfy of all dogs, bore what amounted to no resemblance to the gray, yellow-eyed, rangy presence who was sizing me up at close range. Everything about it said "wolf." And everything about me was saying, "I know you don't like men. Even though I am a man, I am a very nice fellow, and look! Jill is here! Jill likes me. I am nice, see?"

The wolf approached me, turned her head sideways, and bestowed many kisses on my hands. I felt absolutely honored, beyond any other possible tribute. Then the wolf, predictably, threw herself on Jill as though Jill were her long-lost mother.

We left that place in a state of perfect happiness. When we got home, and our dogs sniffed the wolf spit on my hands, I achieved status I have never before enjoyed in my own house.

Chapter 28

The wolf's name was Matilda. She was an eighteen-year-old timber wolf. Ten years earlier she had been retired from the National Zoo when the wolf pack there had rejected her. The other wolves had kicked her out because she was slightly cross-eyed, we were told.

Naturally, we went to see her a second time. Jill brought peanut-butter-flavored dog biscuits.

"I doubt if she'll accept those," said the female of the wolf-owning couple. "She's completely a creature of habit, and a very picky eater."

I need hardly say that the wolf was mad for the peanut-butter biscuits, cadged one after another—most of which she hid behind her doghouse—and wound up stealing the whole bag, which Jill had hung on a branch about six feet off the ground.

On this visit, I found out the wolf liked me—which honor continues to surpass anything I can think of.

The wolf recognized us, which is typical of wolves.

They learn things in one go and never forget them. It stands to reason—in the case of a predator making its living in the wild, slow-witted individuals are going to be dropped from the gene pool pretty early on.

We instantly picked up the topic of our last discussion, which was how Matilda is a wolf, and nobody should mistake her for one of the mere dogs she kennels with. This seemed to be a theme with her, and with other wolves I've met and heard tell of. They don't want to be taken for humans either. Being a wolf, and having everybody know they are, is what they're all about.

She started out by expressing interest in my camera bag.

"What's this, a bag? I like bags. It's my bag now. I can have it if I want, because I'm a wolf."

She exposed her teeth, which were sufficiently impressive close up to cause me a momentary wave of dizziness, and pretended to be gnawing at the corner of the bag.

"I can rip this open, you know. There isn't a thing you can do about it, on account of I'm a wolf."

Accompanying this was a winsome look, wolf-style—which is to say only slightly menacing.

"Nah, I was only kidding. I won't tear your bag. See? I know how to

open it the regular way. You just flip the flap with your nose."

So saying, she flipped it and rooted around with her long snout. "What's this? Film? Is film good to eat? I bet I can crunch this. I *might* crunch it. If I want to. I'm a wolf, you know. Can do whatever I want."

On the face of it, it seemed inconceivable that she could grasp a concept like "captive wild animal," but some of the conversations documented with Koko the gorilla suggest the idea might not be all that far-fetched. This display of teasing, while good-natured, was making a point. You would only have had to see the sparkle in her eyes.

I bought back my camera bag and uncrunched roll of film from Matilda for a couple of biscuits, and she turned her attention to Jill. If she liked me, she loved Jill. A lot of kissing, licking, and nuzzling went on.

All this time, Jacques and Maxine were watching from the backseat of the car. When we had been playing with some of the Malamutes Matilda lives with, and a bunch of Inuit puppies fresh from the Arctic, our dogs had been animated and interested. When the dogs were put away and the wolf released, I noticed our pair slowly sinking out of sight.

A while later, I went out to the car to check on our dogs and give them biscuits. I offered Jacques one from a hand that still had wolf spit on it. He hung his head and turned away. His expression was wretchedly depressed.

"Please," he said, "don't add to my humiliation. Just take me away from this place as soon as you can."

I found out later that someone had visited the kennel with a chocolate Labrador, and the humans had turned the wolf loose to see what would happen. (I could have told them what would happen, but these were scientists, you see, and needed to find out for themselves.) Matilda feebly limped up to the Lab, saying, "Hold on there, dearie. I'm eighteen. I don't do anything fast."

Whereupon she flipped the Lab on its back and was in position to tear its throat out when they pulled her off.

"*What?* It had floppy ears. It was okay to eat, wasn't it? You bring me stuff, then you won't let me enjoy it. Make up your minds."

Then she creaked and wobbled off to her enclosure like the ancient wolf she was. Ancient. But a wolf.

Chapter 29

Even though our friendship was not to last long, and we met only a few times, Matilda the timber wolf left me with a lot of moments to think about.

To know a wolf was important to me because dogs are important to me, and getting to interact with the ancestral animal fills out some of the spaces in my understanding. I say "interact" rather than "observe" because while I'm interested in the behavior of wolves in the wild, what really attracts me is the idea that at some point their species teamed up with ours.

Dogs and people communicate. That's why we're allies. Sometimes, when I am dealing with a canine, the usual business with body language and facial expressions is going on, and somewhere in my head, what the dog—or, in this case, wolf—is saying gets expressed, or anyway remembered, as having a voice.

So here I was, paying another visit to Matilda. I need to tell you that for a number of years, at any given time,

I have been likely to have had an abdominal wound at some stage of healing—the result of a series of surgeries to repair the work of a Poughkeepsie surgeon about whom I hope you will read in the papers someday.

I had a fresh gash with a surgical dressing under my sweater, and Matilda and I were relating in the usual way—cordial but deferential. Jill was free to ruffle Matilda's fur and chuck her under the chin, hug her even. I was not. Our mode was to sidle up to each other, lean against each other, seemingly unconsciously, maybe a reserved and respectful stroke, maybe a light lick on the hand. We were formal with each other.

This is what Matilda did, and this is what she said.

The long, inquisitive nose went for my side. A gentle nuzzle, and a slurping lick on the sweater, the length of the wound.

And this is the voice of Matilda, as I heard her in my head. "Listen, boychik. I vant to give you a little lick. Don't vorry, I vouldn't bite you. It's a volf ting. It's for luck. Okay? So, you're a nice boy, you should heal and be healthy."

I don't know why I used to hear Matilda with a Yiddish accent. Well, she looked Jewish.

Chapter 30

I have to tell you about the happiest being I have ever encountered. His name is Puggiq, and he is an Inuit dog from arctic Canada. It seems the people who took care of Matilda were into not just sled dogs and wolves but the whole subject of the Arctic, exploration, natural history, culture of the native peoples, culinary delights—they liked the complete package.

Every year they head north and pay a local Inuit to risk their lives. This he does by schlepping them along with him as he goes about his regular errands, which involve sledding out onto the frozen sea, being followed by hungry polar bears, and eating parasite-ridden raw meat. They love it and go back again and again.

Jill and I once found ourselves freezing to death in a tiny tent beside a glacier in Iceland, and while we enjoyed the midnight sun and being in a rocky, desolate, subarctic landscape, we got over it.

It was a different story with Matilda's keepers. Borealis called to them. This time they brought home three of the local dogs, two of them with puppy. Their plan was to add the adults, and maybe a couple of puppies, to their Malamute team, then find homes for the remaining pups. Of course they didn't plan on sixteen puppies, which is how many they got.

Life for a genuine working sled dog in the Arctic is hard and short. If a dog can't contribute, it dies. The Inuit dog handlers have no time for sentiment. Dogs get fed every other day, and if they meet a polar bear, it's up to them to make the best deal they can.

You'd think generations of this sort of experience would produce a sullen or standoffish sort of dog, but when Jill and I flew like arrows to see the puppies as soon as we were told about them, this is what we found:

Puggiq, a very sturdy and athletic dog with a shining, hilarious expression around the eyes, was having some exercise, bounding around the yard, when we arrived. He moved as if he were wearing a new pair of basketball shoes. Immediately, he engaged me in conversation.

"Hey," he said. "Is this Florida or what? I can't believe this place! We get fed each and every day. We don't do *any* work to speak of. Haven't seen a polar bear since we got here—and look at this! This is a doghouse! When it rains, I just go under here, and I don't get rained on. Can you beat it? And look! Look at this! This is a tree! Look what I can do! This is some kind of resort, right?"

Jill had brought along some of her secret weapon for winning the hearts of dogs—those peanut-butter-flavored dog biscuits. She slipped one to Puggiq.

"Peanut butter? You've got peanut butter here? I can't believe it! I don't even know what peanut butter is! This place is great!"

I took a lot of pictures of Puggiq. Not very many came out because he was in constant motion. One of the things he was able to do was fly—or float. As massive and powerful as he was, he could drift up into the air and land on the roof of his doghouse as lightly as if he were filled with helium.

I don't pretend to know everything about sled dogs, but I think I can tell when one moves well. Arnold, and a couple of others I remember, were a joy to behold when they got to covering the ground. These dogs would have appeared downright clumsy beside Puggiq, or any Inuit dog. There wasn't anything fancy about the way he moved—just the opposite. There was complete economy, but with such precision, combined with such bounce, that watching him would cause one to grin broadly—which was what he himself was doing. He danced everywhere he went, except when running . . . then he flew.

Impressive as Puggiq and the two mothers, Tiri and Amaroq, were, it was the puppies we had come to see. Jill had been scouting for a replacement for Arctic Flake for years, and this had the makings of an interesting project.

Tiri's pups, ten in all, had one eye open among them and were still pretty much focused on Mom's teats. Amaroq's six, however, were big and fat and fuzzy, already making forays out of the den. All of them were girls, and turned and wheeled as if they were yoked together—all but one. One puppy had a tendency to travel north-by-northeast when her sisters were going north. When they were all distracted by a leaf or a twig, she was studying something else. At one point, she went on a little excursion that took her right past some enclosures containing Malamutes, and the pen from which Matilda gazed at her noncommittally.

This was, in terms of my experience and study, the puppy not to pick. Independence and originality of thought are regarded, more or less sincerely, as human virtues—you don't really want them in a dog. You want a cooperative pack-oriented animal who will try to fit in. I knew this pup wasn't going to be that. I also knew, within seconds of seeing her, that this was the one Jill was going to choose.

Chapter *31*

I had sworn I would not become like other dog trainers, but it is inevitable—you get so you are able to communicate with a dog or two, and you think you can train anything. At the height of my arrogance, I would have taken on a Tasmanian devil or a Komodo dragon.

We listened politely to a raft of advice about how these Inuit dogs were not meant to be kept as pets. The idea was that they'd go to people whose hobby was dogsledding, where they'd add speed and vigor to teams of Malamutes and huskies. (When it came to it, they also taught the Malamutes a few things about toothwork and treachery, thus making a favorable impression.)

Only because of our extensive knowledge and experience, and the fact that the puppy we wanted had flunked the personality test administered by a professional puppy evaluator (assuming there is such a thing), did the breeders allow us to purchase little Lulu.

After at least three thousand years, and as many as ten thousand years of breeding to a single purpose, with a practice of culling not just undesirable dogs but any dog for which there was no immediate use, Inuits were honed to a keen edge, we were told. Put a harness on any one of them and it would more or less know what to do. What it didn't know, the older dogs would teach it—and all the human had to do was establish that he deserved respect and toss the dogs some food every second or third day. But housebreak one—had it ever been done? Get one so it could be left alone with one's possessions? They are quick of tooth, dangerous to life and limb when in a group, incessantly and unbearably noisy when happy, and worse when something is bugging them.

I couldn't wait to get away from the know-it-alls at the kennel so Jill and I could begin to work our magic on the lovable lump of clay that was Lulu. After all, we had written—in a book, yet—that environment takes precedence over heredity, and what happens to a puppy is more important and has greater impact than what sort of puppy it happens to be: one more example of how it is possible for a human to look right at something and think he is seeing something else. Or, put another way, that which I have just disclosed could stand as a dictionary definition of hubris.

But at an earlier time, I hadn't been so enthusiastic. When Jill had decided she'd waited long enough for Arctic Flake's reincarnated essence to find its way to us under its own power, I told her, "I have a secret bank account. I have more than a thousand dollars salted away."

"So? Why are you confessing this all of a sudden?" she asked.

"How would you like to have a really fancy German shepherd . . . from Europe . . . with three names, the middle one being 'Von'? I'm talking about papers, diplomas, certificates from special courses. The dog comes with a little plaid suitcase containing all its documents, and it understands three or four languages."

"What fun would that be?"

"It's no work. The dog comes pretrained. It has better ancestors than we do. It will be useful. We'll be able to send it out to get the newspaper. It can pick up the dry-cleaning. It can take phone messages."

"Not interested," Jill said. "I need something arctic and wolfy."

"And why is that?"

"For laughs. Sled dogs are funny. Whenever we've had one, it's given me a little chuckle or two every day."

"I grant you they're natural clowns, but wouldn't you say they appeal to a primitive sense of humor?" I asked.

"Am I addressing the author of *The Werewolf Club Meets Dorkula*? You're not exactly Noël Coward, you know."

"Aside from somebody's term paper written at Frobisher Junior College, and an article about a DNA study under way to find out if they're dogs or domesticated wolves, not much is known about this breed. Wouldn't that be a negative factor if we were rational?"

"They're dogs," Jill said. "We're trainers. We could train a Tasmanian devil if we had to."

This happens to people who are married for a long time. They compound their stupidity. And so, with a shiny new travel crate on the backseat of Jill's spectacular old 7-series BMW, soon to be traded for a station wagon so we could carry all our dogs, we set out for Connecticut and high adventure.

Chapter 32

Lulu's first car ride went practically without mishap. She did toss her kibble about halfway home, but that was to be expected—it was a long ride—and before and after the awkward moment, she exhibited considerable composure.

The next stop was the vet's, another experience she'd never had before. She took this in stride too, including injections. Although she hadn't had extensive contact with humans, she appeared to enjoy herself at the veterinary clinic. She was friendly, if self-contained.

It was nearly dark when we got home. Lulu had been doing unfamiliar things, in unfamiliar places, with unfamiliar people, and without her mother or sisters, for most of the day. We had attached a light leash and collar, which she got used to at the vet's, and were able to lead her into the barn, where she met Lokkur, an Icelandic gelding then pushing thirty years of age. Lulu sat down in front of the horse and looked up at him.

Lokkur leaned down and took her tiny muzzle between his lips. She continued gazing up into his eyes as he sucked her nose—an arctic greeting of some sort, for all I know. They were friends from that moment, and to the end of Lokkur's life.

I haven't said what Lulu looked like. She had an ornate set of markings. White legs and underside, a mantle of blue-gray looking like an ink wash in a Japanese brush drawing, a pronounced monocle around her left eye, and a dot on top of her head suggesting a whale's blowhole, and regarded as a sign of luck. Her expression was composed and mostly serious, but her eyes were bright. She had the whitest possible teeth and the most perfect scissors bite. The vet said Lulu was the healthiest puppy she had ever seen, notwithstanding when the lab work came back, the results showed that Lulu was harboring parasites never before seen in these parts—likely picked up from some marine mammal eaten by her mother.

Around eight P.M. I came down to the kitchen and found Lulu sleeping between Jacques and Maxine. Jill was at the kitchen table making a list of what Lulu had experienced that day:

Left mother and littermates
Rode in car
Examined by vet, had injections
Nose sucked by horse
Met two big dogs not related to her

Learned to go up and down stairs
Learned her name
Housebreaking begun

This was too easy! All the admonitions had been the usual breeders' hoo-raw. Here was an intelligent and unusually cooperative puppy. Between our enlightened choice of the very best of the litter and the force of our own personalities, we had this pup just about integrated, and we hadn't had her home a whole day.

If I had understood anything about this kind of dog, I would have known that Lulu had been doing the hardest day's work of her life, memorizing, sizing up, weighing alternatives. Intelligent she surely was . . . cooperative, maybe not so much.

Formerly, I thought instinct could be expressed as follows: "I feel a vague irrational prompting to engage in a certain behavior I don't understand, and I don't know why. So, I find myself building a nest, whatever that is, for whatever incomprehensible reason."

After living with Lulu, I think instinct is more like this [Lulu, while watching the documentary *Nanook of the North* on television]: "Hey, look! See that? The Eskimo in the film seems to have caught a seal! It's one of those spotted ones, and it's a female! Those make the very best eating! Jill! Daniel! When you go to the market, that is the exact animal you should look for! Hey! Are you paying attention?"

If I hadn't seen so many proofs, I'd be disinclined

to buy this myself—but it's my belief that Lulu was deferential and cooperative that first day simply because it was the smart thing to do while she took our measure. We still had a lot to learn, and she had a lot to teach us.

Chapter 33

Years ago, a friend of mine once traveled around with a little movie camera making a film of his various friends—a souvenir for himself. He stopped in Hoboken and took impromptu footage of me with Arnold and Juno. A few months later, he was back with his completed reel, and this is what I saw when my scene came up:

The front door of our building on Hudson Place. The door flies open, and the two dogs and I emerge. It so happens I am wearing a black sweater, smoking a thin cigar, and needing a shave—think of a fat Clint Eastwood. The dogs burst out—Juno looks right and Arnold looks left, then they each look the other way. I too am looking up and down the street, shifty-eyed.

We are all looking for the same thing, but for different reasons. Arnold is looking for his hated dog-rival, Jolly, in hopes of killing him. I am looking for Jolly in hopes of preventing Arnold from killing him. Juno is looking for Jolly anticipating that Arnold will want to kill him, I will try to prevent it, and she will help whomever appears to be winning. This is the sled dog's idea of comedy.

One night soon after, Jill and I were out with the dogs. I had stepped into the Erie Lackawanna station and bought two Styrofoam cups of coffee. We were drinking our coffees by the statue of Sam Sloan, in the cobbled plaza in front of the station, when Jill suddenly vanished into thin air.

This was instanta-neous. I remember the cup of coffee seemed to hover sus-pended for a long moment, with Jill and Arnold, both of them, completely gone . . . trans-ported by aliens.

It was one of those slowed-down-time experiences. As the cup of coffee hit the cobblestones, I had turned my head fast enough to see the soles of Jill's sneakers disappear under the swinging doors of Duke's House, an antique saloon situated a few yards from the Sam Sloan statue.

My cup hit the cobblestones next as Juno and I lit out after her.

What had happened was this: Arnold had seen a dog he thought was Jolly, in Duke's House under the swinging doors. Arnold was after him like a flash and dragged Jill behind him. The leash was twisted around her wrist, but Jill isn't the letting-go kind anyway.

It was not Jolly. It was Jolly's brother. Arnold screeched to a stop. "You're not him! What goes on here?" Chances were Arnold would have jumped him anyway, but his hesitation gave Jill a chance to scramble to her feet, and I burst through the swinging doors with Juno, and together, the three of us dragged Arnold back outside.

From the standpoint of the men drinking in Duke's House, and Jolly's brother, the scene must have been as abrupt and inexplicable as Jill's disappearance had appeared to me mere seconds before.

Malamutes who live together like to get drunk and have a fight every Saturday night. Since they don't have a means of getting drunk, they just fight. These encounters can be chilling to the observer. There are deep growls, raised hackles, flying ropes of saliva, and pow-

184

erful bodies fully engaged from the snarling muzzle to the base of the flailing tail.

However, when we would pull Juno and Arnold off each other, the damage tended to be minimal or symbolic—a puncture through a paw or the nose, or maybe a little cut on the cheek just below the eye, which would leave a distinguished scar so other dogs would get the idea.

These encounters took place quite regularly—sometimes when we had guests. We'd hear the familar guttural sounds and jump up just in time to drag the dogs off each other, their faces contorted in horrible snarls. I had sunk a ringbolt into the masonry on either side of the living room, and we kept a short length of chain attached. We'd clip the dogs to the chains and be back in our seats, ready to continue the conversation in half a minute. But often our guests were pale or nauseated— and in need of a breath of air, or wanting to go home and never visit again.

I mention these things now, in the middle of Lulu's story, because Inuit dogs are much stronger, much faster, and much more talented at doing evil things than Malamutes are. They are not evil in themselves. They are good-natured and capable of jokes in ghastly bad taste.

In the Arctic there have been instances of a team of Inuit dogs viewing a human child as prey. These dogs, who have traditionally been turned loose in summer to fend for themselves, were starved. If Lulu had not been raised as a pet, trained a lot, and fed every day, would she be dangerous in that way?

We assume that she *is* dangerous in that way, as full of love and joy as she is. I love Lulu, and I invite the reader to love her too—but please don't think of seeking a dog like Lulu. Her story isn't over—and I can't guarantee a happy ending.

Chapter **34**

When Lulu hears a sudden loud noise, such as a paper bag inflated and popped, or a bookcase falling over, she runs toward the sound. If you were to shout at her in anger, she would run to you and lean against your legs—generally agreed to be the Inuit dog's version of a hug. If one were to smack her, her body language would convey "Yes, yes! Smack me! I stole the roast beef, and now I get smacked! This is such a good game!" It soon becomes clear that to smack her so that she takes it seriously would be to smack her a lot harder than one is willing to.

After her first day with us, when it became clear to Lulu that we were not going to make her into mittens, she began to manifest her whole personality, not just the favor-currying, sucking-up part.

She could scream. She could scream as though being fed through a shredder, slowly. She could scream so that one would see flashes of color and touch one's ears to feel if there was a trickle of blood. And she could keep it up. This kind of screaming could be brought on by, for example, trying to get her to ride in the car crate. She had two crates (actually wire cages): her sleeping crate, which she liked and would enter voluntarily at bedtime, and the car crate, which she did not like and would set her screaming. She preferred to sit between the two big dogs, and once we allowed that, she was perfectly content. We, of course, had lost a contest of wills with the puppy—something she would keep in mind.

The uncanny lupine single-trial learning continued, but with a tincture. She learned the basic obedience routine in a day—in an hour, really. The next day, she still knew it all perfectly but decided it was for idiots. Marching along, with her nose just ahead of my left knee, strikes her as square, and she will not do it for more than five or six paces.

I have thought of founding the Famous Dog Trainers School. In return for your considerable check, you receive a crate containing . . . Lulu. You then train her in the basic obedience skills according to the booklet stapled to the crate. Every few days, she looks at you, blinking her arresting eyes, and asks, "Heel? Is that something I am supposed to know? Did we cover it in class?" You can perfect your teaching technique over and over, and . . . it's a character builder.

The other day, we were walking in the park where Jacques and I had enjoyed so many marches. A woman passing said, "You're trying to teach her to heel, are you?"

"Yes, madam. I've been trying to teach her to heel for five years."

"You know, there are classes you can go to—maybe they can help you."

I thanked the woman in my best borderline-idiot manner and lurched off, dragged by Lulu.

Lulu is not obedience-oriented. And yet she is a huge success. Her littermates grew up to be holy terrors. Put them in a vehicle and they erupt from every orifice. They fight among themselves like devils. Aqsaq, the other prettiest and brightest puppy in Lulu's litter, would eat her own mother's liver if she could, and she proved this by nearly doing so. (Aqsaq met Lulu on one occasion, and it was possible to read her thoughts off her face. They were: "Look at this! Not a mark on her! Come here, sweetheart—I want to show you something." If Lulu had gotten within reach, I am sure Aqsaq would have tried hard to kill her.)

How did Lulu escape being a complete monster? Of course, not being raised with other Inuit dogs had something to do with it—but Lulu is not only no ruffian, she is deferential, affectionate, tolerates cats, neither fouls the house nor touches our nonedible property. How did she come to be practically domestic? Is it because we are such tuned-in and gifted animal psychologists? Did we employ some advanced and enlightened technique?

It was Maxine! Maxine, the superfluous Labrador

retriever! Maxine, who had a complete knowledge of every routine in the house. Maxine, mostly ignored by me for years as not very interesting. It was Maxine the insanely maternal control freak who made our Lulu fit to live with (within certain limits). Maxine trained her, inculcated what moral qualities she may have, and showed us, by contrast, what a really good dog was.

Maxine was on the puppy's case every minute of every day. Housebreaking was accomplished in record time, by example, and by ratting Lulu out the time or two she was about to make an error. Decorum at mealtimes, keeping one's teeth off the humans' possessions, when to be quiet, when to romp and wrestle, and correct modes of relating to cats—all these were taught and fanatically supervised by Maxine.

In addition, Maxine made herself available as punching bag, chew toy, pillow, and trampoline, siphoning off Lulu's demonic energy and giving the rest of us peace. None of the sled breeds mature fast, and this schooling went on for a year and a half to two years.

Each night, at seven, Maxine would hurl herself onto the couch with a loud sigh. This was to indicate that she was now off duty until the morning. Should the puppy approach, she would be shown a mouthful of teeth. It took only a couple of experiments for Lulu to be convinced that Maxine meant it. For the evening, we had the care of our fatigued and disciplined-to-a-fare-thee-well little darling. Easiest puppy raising we ever drew. It's also an argument for hiring a nanny.

During Lulu's education, Jacques served as role model and pack leader, which did not interfere with the duties he already had, narrowed down to a morning walk with me and sleeping the rest of the day in my office. He didn't really have leadership qualities, but the one time Lulu challenged him—as she had to do, being what she was—he rose to the occasion, roared at her, and put a fang in her nose. She was satisfied and continued to admire him—and all was peace.

Chapter 35

I observed Lulu, at four months of age, frustrated by a shut door. She was not aware, or had forgotten, that I was observing, so there were no histrionics. Nor did she paw and scratch at the door. She sniffed along the bottom. She sniffed up the sides. Then she sat down and looked at it.

She was thinking, "There's usually a mechanism. The metal thing smells of their hands—that's where they touch it." She rose up on her hind legs, balancing with her forepaws against the door, took the doorknob in her jaws, and rattled it experimentally. I got up from where I was sitting and opened the door for her. I didn't want to be a witness to this. I didn't want to see a dog of mine solve the canine equivalent of the Unified Field Theory that the doorknob represents.

Lulu began watching television. It was clear she was following the action on the screen. A big favorite of hers was a documentary about wolves. She had favorite actors, all dominant male wolves. During commercial breaks, she would doze, unless the commercials were about food. A scene she found especially interesting showed a snowmobile pulling a sled in a large open space. Lulu was born in September, came to live at our house in November of a particularly dry winter, and at this point had hardly seen snow, let alone sledding.

As might be expected, the animal channel was her favorite, and she soon learned to sit in front of the turned-off set and insist we turn it on. Lulu also demonstrated a liking for cartoons and children's programs. When someone brought me a doll representing one of the Teletubbies, Lulu went ballistic. She was convinced Tinky Winky had come to see her, and became so excited and noisy that I snuck the doll under my shirt and left it shut in the bathroom. Lulu spent the rest of the night lying in front of the bathroom door, wheezing and whining. Lulu watched the televised Westminister Kennel Club competition and developed a barking, wagging, raving enthusiasm for the papillon, who took best of show.

We wondered if she'd been deceived as to the papillon's size by the TV close-ups, but later she met one in the park and made a fool of herself. It's not uncommon—some big girls like the little fellows.

The scrutiny with which she viewed television prompted an experiment. I wrote the words SIT and DOWN on three-by-five cards. I showed her the first one and spoke the command. She sat, and I gave her a tiny treat. Then I showed her the DOWN card and spoke the command. She complied and got another tiny treat. We did it a few more times, and I dispensed with the commands. Sure enough, Lulu was able to distinguish one card from another and execute what was written, as long as the tiny treats kept coming. When I ran out, she wandered off. Such is the way of the noble northern dog. About a week later, the flash cards turned up again, and I tried them on her. She remembered. I added the command SPEAK to her vocabulary—again, she learned it at once, never forgot it, and would perform only if a reward was visible.

I think it's because of thousands of years of living in a village where everyone knows everyone, but Lulu thinks she knows everyone. What is more, she appears to feel bound by some ancient Inuit courtesy to greet those she knows. When we meet another walker in the park, Lulu's behavior and body language convey, "What do you MEAN, we can't stop to talk because we're working? What does that MEAN? Don't you know we HAVE to talk to every person and every dog? Do you want them to think we're RUDE?"

If she likes people, she loves her vet. When we take her to see Dr. Allan Stanley, she's like a crazed fan at a rock concert. There's screaming and piddling on the floor, and that's before he comes into the exam room. (I know nothing firsthand about piddling on the floor at rock concerts—that's just surmise.) When he does arrive, she stands on her hind feet, stretching to her full height, with one toe on the edge of the table to give her balance. She then spins around and swoons backward into his arms, with her head cocked back, gazing up into his face with a weird expression of joy.

And if she loves Al Stanley, there is no word to express her fanatical excitement when she meets Bill Jameison. Bill is a surgeon with a personality nothing like that of most surgeons—which is to say he has one. He encourages Lulu, which is hardly necessary. In his presence, she is completely out of control.

I have no theories to offer. Lulu is gregarious, likes everybody, and is wild about tiny lapdogs and medical men. I can't opine about how she develops her tastes, except to say that she watches a lot of television.

I was probably closer to Juno and Jacques, but my relationship with Lulu is certainly the most physical one I've had with any dog. She's admirable in her efficient athletic build, and also aesthetically pleasing, clean-smelling, and balletic in her movement. She does a flat-footed stamping dance all around the house, but her feet seem to make no impact, and should she step on your toe (which can only be intentional, precise as she is), it's light as a feather. She can move in all directions at once and is capable of going up a flight of stairs before me, backward, mugging, and nuzzling my face as she ascends. I am told that all Inuit dogs are crazy about hugging, once they find out such a thing is possible, and Lulu is simply the best hugger I have ever known. She has identified a thousand toeholds

around the house, allowing her to stand and embrace one, which she does with her whole body—but there is never any pressure. She curls around you like smoke. Add to this the thrill and the privilege of touching that wild wolf-coat and inhaling that arctic ozone that seems to surround her: It's physical, and it's love. It isn't sex, but that's only because she's a dog.

Chapter 36

Lulu jumped Maxine the other day. It was prompted by nothing one could see. The dogs, Jill, and I were hanging out at one end of the living room, talking. Suddenly Lulu was on Maxine, and Maxine was screaming. I hadn't had to break up a dog fight since the roistering days of Juno and Arnold in Hoboken, but I was on my feet in a second and had the aggressor, Lulu, by the tail. It was a whole lot harder detaching Lulu than it had been with the hundred-pound Malamutes. What was more, I don't think she was really serious, either about resisting me or hurting Maxine. For all the caterwauling, Maxine didn't have a single puncture, although she was upset, heart pounding, breathless. We all were.

I did my best to persuade Lulu that I was genuinely mad at her—maybe she believed me. The critical move was Maxine's, and she handled it to perfection. After doing thirty minutes in isolation and disgrace—agony for a pack-oriented animal—Lulu tried to get Maxine to forgive her. Nothing doing. Maxine kept Lulu on the hook for hours. When Maxine finally gave in, Lulu was a nervous wreck.

The clash was my fault entirely. I ought to have seen it coming and should have prevented it. The reason I didn't: laziness and sloth. I'll explain. The reason Lulu jumped Maxine, whom her quasi-civilized side adores, was probably that Maxine has cancer and is gradually fading away (though symptom-free and having a very good time). But Lulu's primitive pack-dog persona sensed weakness and went to test and exploit it—hence the bullying.

How far the fight would have gone had we not been right there, I can't say. Years ago, Lulu bit Maxine's leg when we weren't on the scene. We got there just after the fact, and Lulu was punished. Maxine was lobbying to have Lulu let back into the house and forgiven, even as we were trying to dress the wound. And for a long time, Lulu exploited Maxine's good nature, shoving her aside when affection or treats were offered, and generally being a boor and a swine until about a year ago, when we discovered that Lulu had received a wound identical to the one she had given Maxine. From that day on, Maxine asserted herself, insisted on getting the same degree of attention as Lulu, the same treats, and the same rights to space. Apparently she had decided that Lulu was grown up and no longer entitled to special puppy privileges.

How was this last outrage my fault? Very simple—I had been favoring a knee injury and had become irregular about taking Lulu to the park for morning training. However much of a deliberate sad sack she is at close-order drill, it's still a ritual reinforcement of those aspects of our roles wherein she is the dog and I am the master. Instead of working out a routine adapted to my limited capacity, I let the whole thing slide and usually substituted a ride on my recumbent Exercycle, leaving Lulu out of the loop.

I knew perfectly well that any dog at all should have regular sessions in which the basics are reinforced, let alone a difficult and, let's face it, dangerous dog like Lulu. I was as much at fault in the Maxine at-

tack as if it had been I who chewed on her legs and got slobber all over them.

Lulu and I have been out working in the morning rain the past two days. She feels better for it, I feel better for it—and we discovered McDonald's has a yogurt offering which probably contains a minimum of beef fat, and which we both like.

As I sat in the car the other day, looking across the Hudson at the hills wreathed in fog, enjoying my yogurt cup with Lulu's chin resting on my shoulder, I thought of the others, the predecessors, all the dogs who had been mine and those I had known and helped to train. Even today, as Lulu indirectly reminded me, so much of my life, so many choices, have been prompted by my relationships with canines.

Born to be the king of the couch potatoes, I probably owe my comparatively robust health to all those dogs who needed to walk and showed me how to enjoy the simple act of moving along the ground. Myopic, interiorized, and slow to notice things, not to mention having been raised surrounded by concrete and on city streets, how did I gain joy in observing nature except by making friends with beings who appreciated it and were part of it?

And raised by two-fisted, bare-knuckle immigrants and gangsters, where was I to find examples of real friendship?

They've been my teachers, this little succession of barkers—they've shown me a lot about how it's possible to live this life, and also how to leave it, loving it right up to the last second.

The cycle will continue for a while. Maxine will go soon, and then . . . oh, God help us . . . when we get the next puppy, it will be Lulu who plays the mother!

About the Author

Daniel Pinkwater is regarded by critics, educators, psychologists, and law enforcement agencies as the world's most influential writer of books for children and young adults. For thirteen years he was a regular commentator on NPR's *All Things Considered,* and two collections of his essays have been brought out to the delight of listeners who can read. He is a regular contributor to NPR's *Weekend Edition Saturday,* and is co-host, with Scott Simon, of *Chinwag Theater,* distributed by WBUR, Boston. He lives in Hyde Park, New York.